MULTICULTURAL
PUBLIC RELATIONS

MULTICULTURAL PUBLIC RELATIONS

A Social-Interpretive Approach

second edition

Stephen P. Banks

Iowa State University Press

Ames, Iowa

STEPHEN P. BANKS, Ph.D., is a professor of communication, School of Communication, University of Idaho, Moscow.

Iowa State University Press
2121 South State Avenue, Ames, Iowa 50014
Orders: 1-800-862-6657
Office: 1-515-292-0140
Fax: 1-515-292-3348
Web site: www.isupress.edu

Authorization to photocopy items for internal or personal use, or the internal or personal use of specific clients, is granted by Iowa State University Press, provided that the base fee of $.10 per copy is paid directly to the Copyright Clearance Center, 222 Rosewood Drive, Danvers, MA 01923. For those organizations that have been granted a photocopy license by CCC, a separate system of payments has been arranged. The fee code for users of the Transactional Reporting Service is 0-8138-2940-2/2000 $.10.

⊛ Printed on acid-free paper in the United States of America

First edition, 1995 © Sage
Second edition, 2000 © Iowa State University Press

Library of Congress Cataloging-in-Publication Data

Banks, Stephen P.
    Multicultural public relations: a social-interpretive approach / Stephen P. Banks.—2nd ed.
        p.   cm.
    Includes bibliographical references and index.
    ISBN 0-8138-2940-2 (alk. paper)
    1. Public relations.   2. Intercultural communication.   3. Multiculturalism.   I. Title.

HM1221 .B35   2000
659.2—dc21   00-040991

The last digit is the print number: 9 8 7 6 5 4 3 2 1

Contents

Preface

Since the first edition of this book appeared in 1995, much has changed in theory and research about public relations. Much has changed as well in the practice of the profession. Academic journals are publishing more rigorous, theory-oriented research than ever before; a number of excellent books that seek to integrate public relations with other social and organizational concerns have appeared recently; and public relations professionals are adopting new technologies and practices that help them keep pace with the dizzying transformations we are witnessing in commerce and the workplace.

Yet in the past half decade, much more in the public relations world has remained the same. It continues to be the case that scant attention is paid in research or practice to the predicaments of culturally diverse populations and the necessity for learning to communicate effectively across cultural differences. It continues to be the case that persons of color are underrepresented at all levels of the profession and that women continue to have expectations of lower pay, slower advancement and less career security than men preparing for the occupation. It continues to be the case that public relations overwhelmingly is negatively portrayed in the news media: A recent study by Julie K. Henderson found public relations characterized in the press as a corrupter of democracy, an obstacle in the communication process, a sleight of hand or a disaster much more often than it was favorably characterized.

These conditions, persisting in a technology-dominated economy that is transforming the ways most people live their public and private lives, have prompted me to prepare a second edition of *Multicultural Public Relations*. This edition brings the previous chapters up to date by referencing current research that is relevant to the various topics. Because the explosive growth of Internet-related media has come to dominate communication in virtually all areas of business and government, I have added a new chapter devoted to the influence of new technologies in multicultural public relations. In the final chapter I have modified somewhat my earlier points on PR education, and I have expanded my earlier perspective on the ethical practice of public relations. Nonetheless, my overall orientation to the field has not fundamentally changed: Public relations still needs stronger theory and a more socially sensitive and meaning-centered communication practice, one that focuses on building positive multicultural relationships and communities.

Many people contributed to the development of this book. My thanks go first to Judi Brown at Iowa State University Press. She has been a cordial, informative and astute colleague in the creation and production of this edition. My special thanks go to Lynne Bishop and Lori Meek Schuldt for careful and thorough editing. I am grateful also for lunchtime discussions with colleagues at the University of Idaho and at Washington State University's Murrow School of Communication—their interest has helped keep me on the course toward completing the work. I wish especially to thank Bonnie Dostall Neff for her commitment to diversity in the practice and teaching of public relations and her willingness to foster discussion of this book. My views also have been enriched by talks with Mike Berriochoa, Tracey Feist and Diane Alverio. As always, my most heartfelt thanks go to Anna Banks, for her gentle encouragement and forbearance: This project wouldn't have happened without her support.

Preface to the First Edition

As an early assignment in my introductory public relations course, I ask students to bring to class "mentions" of public relations they find in the mass media. Over the six years I have been assigning this task, the overwhelming majority of media references to public relations my students encounter are negative, likening public relations communication to deception, whitewashing, manipulation and insincerity.

I use this exercise to make the point that public relations, as a communication occupation and social institution, has a long way to go to achieve legitimacy. In my view, the main reason public relations is so tainted and "preparadigmatic" is its controversial function in society. Public relations literally is born and immersed in controversy—no need for change, no need for public relations. Thus, differences of perspectives are at the very heart of public relations practice.

We need stronger theory to support a more virtuous practice of institutional communication, theory that both recognizes the inevitability of conflict and diversity and contributes to a more just society. The central argument of this book is that only by focusing on the construction of meaning and the values, patterned activities and relationships that shape and are shaped by subjective meanings can public relations be truly effective. The social-interpretive approach to multicultural public relations thus joins diversity of experience and values with the ways we categorize groups of people we see as being different. I believe that taking this broader view of diversity can improve both the theory and the practice of public relations communication.

Although my name alone appears as author of this volume, many people helped me with materials and ideas and provided conversational challenges and encouragement. I am especially indebted to Rocky Barker, Carl Botan, Steve Corman, Jim Fisher, Kerry Flodin, Bill Gudykunst, Ruth Guzley, Dana Horton, Ken Laverty, Esther Louie, Linda Larkey, Kristin Maestas, Terry Maurer, Michelle Posey and Stella Ting-Toomey. I also thank my students and colleagues at the University of Idaho—may we continue to learn from one another. Last, which also comes first, is gratitude to Anna Banks for her support before, during and after this project.

MULTICULTURAL
PUBLIC RELATIONS

CHAPTER 1

Culture, Diversity and Public Relations

> We are living in an age of diversity.
> —Don C. Locke, *Increasing Multicultural Understanding*

A timeless adage reminds us that no two people are exactly alike. Indeed, differences—human and otherwise—are all around us. But in most cases, the ways people are dissimilar turn out to be trivial, and we appropriately ignore those differences. In other cases, we see the dissimilarities among people as significant, and we tend to assign people to categories of difference. These perceived dissimilarities can have immense practical consequences.

This book is about recognizing, analyzing and responding to those perceived categories of human differences that might "make a difference" in the practice and study of public relations. This is no simple task. Theorists, educators and managers have long struggled with the concept of differences (Ainlay, Becker and Coleman 1986) and the difficulties of communicating across cultures (e.g., Alberts 1992; Asante and Gudykunst 1989; Gudykunst 1991; Scollon and Scollon 1995; Varonis and Gass 1985; Gass and Varonis, 1991).[1] Moreover, some influential public relations commentators (e.g., O'Dwyer 1994) openly disparage multicultural communication. It is my hope, however, that by better understanding the influences of diversity on public relations and identifying effective ways people in public relations can respond to social changes, the current and following generations of practitioners will be better equipped to communicate in a rapidly changing world. It also is my hope that the ideas in this book will stimulate further theorizing and research among scholars interested in public relations.

As a simple example of what can happen to a public relations practitioner who is insufficiently aware of cultural differences, consider what happened to David M. Grant. Grant had agreed to conduct a publicity program in the U.S. business and trade press for a high-priced European client. Although he achieved excellent press placements in the right markets, the client was not satisfied. The European manager expected Grant to establish close personal contacts in the targeted industries and media markets and to spend lots of time socializing with those representatives. The client even complained that the agency's expenses were *too low*. Eventually, the client switched agencies, ending an $8,000 per month relationship, because of differing cultural assumptions about how public relations should be conducted. As Grant analyzed his problem, "results notwithstanding, when you're dealing with a foreign culture, you must make sure that your concept of good public relations practice is the same as your client's" (Grant 1988, 48).

Public relations practice is potentially filled with embarrassments, missed opportunities, perplexed clients and inadequate performance that can result from misunderstanding cultural differences. The extent of the field's lack of sensitivity to cultural differences is reflected in a survey of public relations professionals my students and I conducted (Banks 1994). When asked what cultural groups among clients or employees were important to their public relations practice, the majority of practitioners could name none. One respondent said, "Diversity isn't a problem for us. We don't have any diversity here." Diane Alverio tells a story that illustrates similar limitations in client perspectives on diversity. Alverio, president of Blake/Alverio Communications, was requested by a client doing business in Puerto Rico to assist in the client's communication efforts with Puerto Rican publics. When she explained the necessity for communicating in a cultural style that is consistent with the audience's expectations, the client responded by observing that is why the client came to her, a PR professional known as a fluent speaker of Spanish. Alverio explained that she is not Puerto Rican and is uncomfortable translating across cultures in which she has little experience. The client insisted, saying, "What's the difference, it's all Spanish, isn't it?" Alverio astutely circumvented the problem by connecting her client with a practitioner who has roots in Puerto Rican culture. This kind of experience convinces me that practitioners like our survey respondents and Diane Alverio's client need more information about the nature of diversity and a clearer theoretical understanding of cultural variability and what it implies for public relations communication.[2]

Research and theory on diversity in public relations, however, are just beginning to emerge. The Public Relations Society of America (PRSA) has commissioned a monograph about multicultural public relations (Miller 1991) and a book-length annotated bibliography of scholarly and popular writing on communication and culture (Miller 1993). A modest number of academic papers on multiculturalism in public relations have appeared in recent years (e.g., Ekachai 1992; Everett 1993; J. Grunig and White 1992; Kern-Foxworth 1990; Kern-Foxworth and Miller 1992; Morton 1997; Skriloff 1997), as well as work on minorities and the media (e.g., Biagi and Kern-Foxworth 1997). Moreover, a huge literature has appeared over the past decade to convey practical guidance on training for and managing in multicultural work settings (e.g., Fernandez 1991; Kikoski and Kikoski 1996; Thiederman 1991; Trompenaars 1994; Wheeler 1996). It is worthy of note, however, that the largest institutionally funded public relations research study, the IABC Research Foundation's "excellence project" (J. Grunig 1992; Dozier, L. Grunig and J. Grunig 1995), contains no direct acknowledgment of multicultural principles or problems, either in what its authors advance as theoretical statements or in applications of the study's findings to professional practice. In the two chapters on societal cultures in those two volumes, the approach taken to diversity is to speculate on how a systems view of symmetric communication can be carried out within differing national cultures. In fact, to date, no comprehensive, theory-driven and systematic treatment of multicultural communication in public relations has appeared.

This book seeks to fill that gap in three ways. It re-examines the nature of culture, diversity, public relations and communicative effectiveness; it establishes a broad-based and culture-sensitive theory of communication for public relations; and it analyzes the influence of different cultural perspectives on public relations practice in internal communications, community relations, activist communication, the uses of new technologies and international programs.

Unfortunately, little agreement exists on how to define even the most fundamental concepts in multicultural public relations. As illustrations of this conceptual uncertainty, consider the following. Debra Miller (1991, 2), referring to the American demographic landscape, remarks: "Some say we should call it multiculturalism, or cultural pluralism. . . . Or is it a salad? A mosaic? A patchwork quilt? A spicy gumbo?" Similarly, Lustig and Koester (1999) describe four metaphors for U.S. cultural diversity—the melting pot, the tributary, the tapestry and the garden salad—none of which, they say, adequately captures the phenomenon. In addition, numerous scholars have commented on the profusion of definitions for culture (e.g., Lustig and Koester 1999, 37; Gudykunst 1991, 42). Dean Kruckeberg and Kenneth Stark (1988, 11), like many other writers on public relations, remark on the "seemingly infinite number of definitions . . . of public relations" (see also Hutton 1999). To help sort out this confusing surfeit of perspectives, I develop in this chapter definitions of three concepts that are central to this

book—culture, diversity and public relations. In the process of exploring
these concepts, I also discuss the encompassing and controversial issue of
how public relations practitioners might think about and engage cultural diversity.

Before proceeding to definitions, however, it will be useful to explore a
crucial phenomenon—the immense variation among the populations of
our world and the unprecedented speed with which social groupings are
changing. (In line with other scholars studying diversity, such as Philomena
Essed, Louise Lamphere and Ashley Montagu, I refer to distinctive groups
of persons as *populations,* or *population groups,* rather than as *minorities, races*
or *ethnic groups,* unless those latter terms are specifically called for by the discussion.) The diversity of populations and the pace and direction of demographic, technological and social change are prime reasons to study multicultural public relations in the first place, and they constitute one of the two
core justifications for this book. The other core justification is the increased
communication demands on organizations brought by populations unified
on the basis of identity politics and special-interest activism.

Changing Populations

Broadly speaking, two types of situation are of concern to U.S. multicultural public relations: communicating with domestic publics and communicating with various publics outside the United States. These two contexts
are identified because of differences in their population dynamics, differences in their public relations objectives and relationships, and differences
in their relevant cultural factors. Both these categories include audiences
comprised of public relations employees and other internal stakeholder publics of organizations as well as a wide range of external publics. This scheme,
depicted in Table 1.1, represents the structure of topics in this book.

In the following discussion, I address first the domestic scene and then
the dynamics of population changes internationally.

Domestic Trends

Practically every observer agrees that the U.S. work force is undergoing dramatic changes demographically. Few recognize, though, just how profound
those changes are. Between 1980 and 1990, the Census Bureau reports, the
U.S. work force grew by about 18 percent; the total population increased by

Table 1.1   Contexts of Multicultural Public Relations

	Domestic setting	International setting
Internal Publics	Local/regional/national employee groups, employee families, investors, and other stakeholders within the United States	Employee groups, employee families, volunteers, investors, and other stakeholders outside the United States
External Publics	Clients, media, opinion leaders, activists, government officials, and others within the United States	Clients, media, opinion leaders, activists, government officials, and others outside the United States

only about 10 percent, however, indicating higher rates of worker partici-pation in the job market. White worker participation increased by 12 per-cent during the decade, yet African-American rates of participation in the work force were up by 23 percent, while rates for Hispanics increased 67 percent, Asian and Pacific Islanders by 106 percent, and American Indians, Aleuts and Eskimos by 45 percent (Bovee 1993). This trend appears to have continued throughout the 1990s (Len-Ríos 1998). Moreover, the Bureau of Labor Statistics projects that by the year 2006, over 27 percent of the U.S. labor force will be comprised of ethnic minorities. While the overall num-bers of workers will increase by about 21 percent between 1990 and 2005, the numbers of African-Americans will further increase by almost 32 per-cent, Asians by over 74 percent, Hispanics by over 75 percent, and women age 55 and older by 54 percent. Marilyn Loden and Judy B. Rosener (1991) report that more than 75 percent of the 24 million new jobs expected to be created between 1990 and 2010 will go to women and nonwhites.

These changes in the workplace are consistent with patterns of change occurring in the entire U.S. population. Using then-current Census Bureau figures, Kelvin Pollard (1993, 3) reports that "the nation is expected to be-come more diverse, older, and substantially more populous than previously thought." What Pollard calls the "racial/ethnic mix" will continue to grow more diverse, resulting in a declining share of the total population by non-Hispanic whites from 76 percent to about 53 percent by about 2050. As I write this chapter, in October 1999, the news media have announced that the population of California no longer has a majority racial or ethnic group—no population in California now has more than 50 percent share of the total.

In addition, the nonwhite populations are expected to grow increasingly diverse: African-Americans will comprise over 15 percent of the U.S. total population by 2050, up from 12 percent today; sometime around 2010, Hispanics will pass African-Americans as the largest non-Anglo group, reaching more than 24 percent of the population in 2050; during the same period, Asians will increase by more than fivefold, comprising more than 10 percent of the total population in 2050.[3]

These trends are not limited to race, ethnicity and gender. Jennifer Lach (1999, 2) reports that "an 'age diversity' movement will grip corporate America by 2025." The Census Bureau projects a 90 percent increase in the general population of persons age 61 to 79 by 2025, when they will make up 19 percent of the total population. The growing age diversity in workplaces will contribute to increased attention to age discrimination issues, Lach predicts, and it will have enormous impacts on customer relations as well: "Companies will start to see 'age diversity' as important as racial or ethnic diversity, critical to staying in touch with all of their customers."

Potentially more important than these demographic trends, however, are recent social trends in the United States. The so-called culture wars refers in part to the fragmentation of the larger society into groups of persons who come together as self-proclaimed cultures, coalescing around a shared view of a social issue or institutional action. The problem for analysts, which will be discussed in more detail later, is how to reconcile the traditional view of diversity, which is based on demographic differences, and the new and insistent elements of diversity, which are based on differences of group perception of self-identity and issues.

International Trends

Beyond the U.S. borders, other demographic changes are evident. The United Nations Population Division of the Secretariat forecasts a continuing rise in world population of 1.7 percent a year, resulting in an increase from 6 billion people today to 8.5 billion in 2025 ("World population" 1992). More important, Debra Miller (1991, 3) reminds us that "few nations today are not multiethnic." The diversity among populations in other lands is intensified by at least four other factors in addition to mere population increases:

1. population migrations and guest worker policies (Victor 1992)
2. the internationalization—some would say the globalization—of business (Cheney 1999; Fitzpatrick 1992)
3. the development of regional trading blocs, such as the European Community (Corbett 1992) and blocs within the EC
4. changes in communication technology and public policy (Hiebert 1992; Neff 1998)

These factors all contribute to an international setting that daily grows more complex for public relations communicators.

In Chapters 3 through 7 I discuss further these changing patterns of domestic and international demographics and their implications for multicultural communication in public relations. Exploring those implications, however, must begin by establishing a common understanding of the nature of culture.

Culture and Multiculturalism

In a pivotal study published more than 40 years ago, Kroeber and Kluckhohn (1952) identified in the research literature 160 different definitions for culture. Although they were able to group those definitions into six basic categories and generate a comprehensive single definition for culture, countless new definitions have been added since then, and today there is still no agreement among scholars about how to conceptualize culture (Collier and Thomas 1988, 102; Gudykunst 1991, 42). What seems important, however, is to identify those elements most scholarly definitions have in common and those phenomena and processes most nonspecialists have in mind when they think about and refer to culture.

Culture as Meaning Systems

Contemporary uses of the term indicate that culture has something to do with the ways a group of people make sense of their experience and differentiate their sense making from other groups' ways of understanding. This view derives from Harry Triandis's (1972) notion of "subjective culture," a term he used to refer to a group's unique way of experiencing its social environment. As such, culture is minimally a set of (usually implicit) theories held in common about how social life works and recipes about how social life is conducted. Some writers, such as William Gudykunst (1991) and Ward Goodenough (quoted in Geertz 1973, 11), interpret this characteristic of culture as a "system of knowledge." But much of what is cultural consists of explanations and actions that are either taken for granted or assumed to be natural or unnoticeable; moreover, it's a commonplace occurrence for people to distinguish between knowing about something or how to do it, on the one hand, and understanding why something should be done or what its doing constitutes, on the other hand (see Geertz 1973, 10–13). Consequently, equating culture with knowledge is less satisfactory than thinking of culture as systems of *meaning* differentially available to groups of people. It is possible to know, for example, how to invite a business associate to dinner in your home in India—to know the ritual of invitation and the rules about seating, dress, gifts, salutations, conversation and farewells; it is even possible to "know" the type of reciprocal commitments implied by inviting a business contact in India to be entertained in your home (see Wouters 1991). What is cultural, however, is the lived experience of an event within which it is the natural thing to do and by which a logic of relationships is maintained.

Acquisition of Culture

If culture is not something explicitly learned as knowledge, it cannot be "picked up" or taught in the sense that we teach the procedures of another group's behavior or the facts about their beliefs. Instead, culture, as Lustig and Koester (1999) point out, is learned in the sense of gaining understandings that are "handed down" in group experience; it is transmitted through interaction with socializing agents. James Paul Gee (1992, 113) distinguishes between two ways of gaining competence, *learning* and *acquisition*:

> *Acquisition* is a process of [understanding] something by exposure to models, a process of trial and error, and practice within social groups, without formal teaching. It happens in natural settings that are meaningful and functional in the sense that acquirers know that they need to acquire the thing they are exposed to in order to function and that they in fact want to so function.... *Learning* is a process that involves conscious knowledge gained through teaching (though not necessarily from someone officially designated a teacher) or through certain life experiences that trigger conscious reflection. This teaching or reflection involves explanation and

analysis, that is, breaking down the thing to be learned into its analytic parts. It inherently involves attaining, along with the matter being taught, some degree of metaknowledge about the matter.

Gee observes that most of what we know and understand is derived from a mixture of acquisition and learning, and some cultures emphasize one mode over the other. But he points out that acquisition facilitates performance while learning leads to discursive knowledge—the ability to talk about, analyze and explain things. More important, cultural practices that constitute the social groupings people live within (what Gee calls "Discourses") are mastered through acquisition, not learning. As Gee explains, "Discourses are not mastered by overt instruction (even less so than languages, and hardly anyone ever fluently acquired a second language sitting in a classroom), but by enculturation ('apprenticeship') into social practices through scaffolded and supported interaction with people who have already mastered the Discourse . . . " (114).

This view of enculturation is consistent with the notion of communication cultures, which "exist when a group of people has understandings of goals and strategies of talk that are not shared by those outside the group and when these understandings are routinely inculcated in new members of the culture" (Wood 1997, 10). Julia Wood links communication cultures to standpoint theories, which hold that the meanings available to a group are constrained, conditioned and mediated by that group's symbolic practices, that is to say, by their Discourses (see Denzin 1997; Wood 1997). Norman Denzin, quoting Dorothy Smith, writes, "This argument is foundational. It challenges the very 'notion of a single standpoint from which a final overriding version of the world can be written'" (1997, 55). Thus, cultures are subjective relationships that are grounded in available meanings through communicative practices.

Does this mean that persons outside a culture will forever remain outside? Not necessarily, for people of any age and origin can undergo enculturation; it does mean, however, that one cannot learn to master performances within a culture simply through explicit teaching. The central implication of this approach to culture is that understanding culture, either as performer within a culture or as observer from outside a culture, requires the matching of meanings and contexts, where "context" refers to the real-world settings in which people go about the performances of their everyday lives and an understanding of their standpoints on those settings and performances.

The Scope of Culture

Two final issues on the definition of culture: First, if culture is to be defined as *systems of meaning group members acquire through experiential apprenticeship*, how can we come to know the boundaries and differences among cultures? Second, and related to the first, what is a cultural unit? That is, how large is a culture and what categories of groups comprise cultures?

Some theorists employ the concept of subcultures to account for the fact that while many aspects of social life are shared among people, other important distinguishing characteristics can be identified for almost any group. The problem with the subculture idea is that it yields endless possibilities for subdividing any cultural group; therefore, the conceptual boundary line must be arbitrarily drawn by the analyst or outside observer (Lustig and Koester 1999). On the other hand, if Geertz's notion of culture as public systems of meaning holds true, then culture is not a set of formulas that exist in people's minds or objective traits groups display. Instead, it is a set of practices that people perform with the logics that attach to those practices that make them sensible. Insofar as these practices are born anew each time a person acts, culture is a living process—"action which signifies" (Geertz 1973, 10)—whose boundaries and terms are subject only to the definitions given them by their practitioners.

Consequently, the question of what are the boundaries and differences among cultures (and subcultures, for that matter) is moot: Cultures are bounded by the ways people make sense of events in their real-world settings, from standpoints that they consensually define. The differences between cultures are not so much matters of different rituals or different gestural signals or different modes of dress, although these elements can be *clues* to cultural differences; they are matters of what people believe they are doing when engaging in their normal, everyday practices. Thus, a culture is as large or small as the group whose ways of constructing meaning about any salient practice are cohesively and homogeneously defined. It is the saliency of a particular practice that determines the cultural boundary of concern to public relations communicators.

Thus, in the perspective on culture I am advocating here, the cultural unit is any group of people who identify themselves in some ways as distinctive or who are so identified by others *in relation to a particular practice or concept*. In many cases, such identification aligns with geographic origin or nationality, as when a person says she is Scandinavian or French; in some cases, it aligns with religion, ethnicity, sex or some other relevant characteristic. (Recently groups of residents in the U.S. Northwest have been claiming that timber workers are a culture, as their traditional livelihoods have become threatened by environmentalist challenges to timber harvest practices in national forests. They arguably are cultural in relation to this particular issue.) In some cases, identification as a cultural group member involves several categories, such as the blending of nationality, race and religion when the Dalai Lama says he is Tibetan. Feminist standpoint theorists argue that categorizing an individual to a single-dimensioned culture is absurdly essentialist: Social lives are multidimensional and plastic, and their stories have many voices of their own choosing (Trinh 1991, 188). The point is that fundamental to a practical understanding of culture is recognizing that culture and its concerns are immaterial if it were not for the simple fact that people see differences among populations with respect to particular concerns and array those differences as distinguishing traits for purposes of group and self-identity.

The Multiculturalism Debates

Strong objections have been raised in recent years against the notion that perceived group differences should be a factor in public life. One writer (Costello 1993), for example, asks that if some groups are identified as specifically protected against discrimination, why shouldn't "Big White Guys with Dark Hair" also be singled out for protection? Barely a notch up the scale of credibility and seriousness is Irving Kristol's (1991) argument that "multiculturalism is a desperate—and surely self-defeating—strategy for coping with the educational deficiencies, and associated social pathologies, of young blacks." Profoundly more challenging than these superficial arguments against multiculturalism is Arthur Schlesinger Jr.'s book, *The Disuniting of America* (1992). Schlesinger pleads elegantly from a classical liberal position that the distinctive historical experience of all Americans should be the focus of policy and social practices. His fear is that multiculturalism in "E Pluribus Unum" emphasizes the "pluribus" over the "unum."

Charles Taylor (1992; see also Gutman 1994) insightfully analyzes the controversy over multiculturalism as one that swirls around subtle incompatibilities within the "politics of recognition." Identity and self-worth, he says, are grounded in the positive recognition given by others. When recognition is withheld, or is given but conveys a negative evaluation, individuals' self-image and identity with their group suffer and they cannot participate equally and fully in society. The politics of recognition is about achieving efficacy in society by being validated as worthwhile, both as individuals and as members of distinctive populations. This confirmation of a society's members appears to be a universal need; in the history of "north Atlantic" liberalism, however, the politics of recognition has been pulled in two incompatible directions. One direction follows Jean-Jacques Rousseau's philosophy toward a politics of equal dignity, whereby persons are accorded equal rights under a "difference-blind" criterion for membership in society. This is the unification impulse that moves Schlesinger to advocate pursuit of the values and traditions that have unified the populations of the United States since the first invasion of this continent by Europeans.

The other direction more explicitly recognizes the modern idea of identity and leads to a politics of difference. This view acknowledges that every person must be recognized for her or his uniqueness, and each person's cultural heritage merits respect as a first principle. The public policies that elaborate the politics of difference recognize unequal socioeconomic conditions people are born into, and this recognition justifies social action to redress those inequalities. The more radical view of the politics of difference says that any evaluation by the dominant culture of the conditions, needs or culture of less fortunate populations is just an expression of the dominant group's ethnocentricity (see Ravitch 1990 and Asante and Ravitch 1991 for debates on this viewpoint). The more radical view of the politics of equal dignity says that any effort to inject elements of others' culture into the history, education or public life of society is an attack on the Western tradition and will undermine the stability and unity of society (see works by Alan Bloom, Dinesh D'Souza and Eric Hirsch in defense of this perspective).

What does the subjective-meaning approach to culture I have outlined say about the debate between these two positions on multiculturalism? Its main contribution is to confront the assumption of objectivity: If culture is subjectively defined, there is no possibility of judging cultural superiority and inferiority. Communicators therefore are freer to recognize differences among populations while confirming others' identities in institutional communication. It also makes it possible for organizations to work toward unifying varieties of populations they wish to communicate with while recognizing the differences that make cultural communication necessary. These advantages fit nicely with Taylor's conclusion that we must seek a position that is "midway between the inauthentic and homogenizing demand for recognition of equal worth . . . and the self-immurement within ethnocentric standards." It is necessary, as Kruckeberg and Stark (1988) argue, to reposition public relations as an institutional effort to re-establish a sense of community, emphasizing commonalities while communicating across differences.

More will be said in Chapter 2 about identity, culture and communication; here, however, it is important to note that the popular term for acknowledging differences among groups of people is *diversity,* and an understanding of diversity will help illuminate the issue of multiculturalism and group boundaries. The following section develops an interpretation of diversity that expands our usual thinking about what categories of people the term encompasses while it softens the often hard boundaries government regulations place on group identities. Ultimately what practitioners and regulators alike need is a sense of diversity that is capable of encompassing any relevant differences among populations.

Reframing Diversity

Because *diversity* is the name of an abstract quality, the term can easily be a proxy for many concepts. Consider these different views. In his poem "From the Crest," Wendell Berry (1977, 47) calls diversity "the great song . . . the braided song," and he portrays it as a force that equally invigorates all living things. The physicist Freeman Dyson (1988, 91) argues that an open, more varied culture and economy have a robustness that more closed systems do not have. To the United States government, race and skin color have been the core properties of diversity since earliest days (Lott 1993), so that currently the U.S. census data have the following categories for persons: White, Black, American Indian/Alaskan Native, Asian/Pacific Islander, Black-not of Hispanic origin, White-not of Hispanic origin, and Hispanic (U.S. Office of Management and Budget Directive 15, cited in Lott 1993).

But is diversity, in the sense it currently is used in discussions about human differences, simply a matter of multiplicity, as Berry celebrates it? Or is it an objective quality of system openness? Or a limited set of categories of racial or ethnic types? While each of these views has merit in its own context, often these diverse perspectives have hampered the debate about how a society or profession should conceive of and engage diversity and have allowed us to gloss over the more sinister underside of the term.

After all, what counts as diversity for purposes of formulating public policy and instituting social action is itself historically and culturally conditioned (G. Becker and Arnold 1986). For example, U.S. government mandates require accommodation in public buildings and workplaces for persons with physical disabilities. In Papua New Guinea, however, such government mandates are absent; the cultural norm is that persons with disabilities make their own accommodation to physical obstacles. In the United States, the constitutional rights of older citizens are believed to be so threatened that legislation is needed to protect them; in much of Asia, however, elders are so honored that special legal protections would be considered ludicrous. Legislation expressly protecting persons against employment discrimination on the basis of sexual orientation would have been unthinkable in the United States as recently as 40 years ago. Even the meaning of the term *equality* in the United States has evolved historically from interaction among different populations, especially between whites and blacks (Condit and Lucaites 1993). This historical and cultural conditioning of what we believe constitutes diversity tells us that the nature of recognizable difference will change over time. Thus, a set of principles and practices that are not category specific is needed to conceptualize and treat diversity.

Diversity as Stigma

In its most basic sense, *diversity* means difference, which derives from the Latin *divertere*, to turn in different directions, or to move apart. But *diversity,* as it is used when talking about culture, refers to not just any divergence: The underlying semantic heritage of the term tells us that the differences that "make a difference" are the factors that separate people, those by which people see themselves as being differently placed and endowed in society. As such, diversity carries an undertone of separateness, a tension grounded in disharmony and inequality, indicating by group characteristics where any individual stands vis-à-vis members of other groups.

That is so because group and self-identity are based on our perceptions of similarities and differences (Gudykunst 1991): I am who I am in large measure because of the groups I am part of, and my group is what it is in virtue of its being different from other identifiable groups. Tajfel and Turner (1979) argue, however, that in-groups are typically characterized by positive characteristics while out-groups and their members usually are assigned negative traits, as the contrast media by which we maintain our own self- and group identities (see also H. Becker 1963). These differences also imply stigmatization—persons who are seen as different are in some way not normal.[4] And here's the rub: While both theorists and practitioners avoid recognizing or discussing it, diversity frequently connotes differences between the culturally normal and the deviant while masquerading as a neutral-sounding cover term for adjustment to social change. Thus, nearly all the prescriptive management literature on diversity focuses on training culturally normal persons how to appreciate the special needs and perspectives of those who are "diverse" and how to adjust the system to accommodate "them" or how to help them adapt. But rarely is the dominant system itself challenged so that fundamental changes to values, goals or social arrangements are made possible (see, e.g., Fernandez 1991; Geber 1990; Loden and Rosener 1991; Thiederman 1991; Thomas 1991, 1996). Frederick Lynch (1997) traces the evolution of the diversity concept in management training from a narrowly defined spectrum of differences to a more varied set of theories and assumptions today that include appreciating, celebrating and negotiating differences among members of a work force.

One problem with this formulation of diversity, of course, is that the definition of what constitutes normality remains in the control of the economically and politically privileged population; thus, immigrants to the United States from Europe are typically defined as part of "us" and not countable as representatives of "diversity," while poor persons fleeing political persecution in Latin America or Asia are marked as "them" and counted as targets of diversity programs (Lott 1993). Moreover, stigma is extremely intractable, and reversing stigma requires major sociocultural movements, such as the women's liberation and civil rights movements (Becker and Arnold 1986).

When diversity is used as a mask for stigmatized difference, it presents policy-makers and managers with the dilemma of how to treat target populations under diversity programs: If those other populations are truly empowered, the whole social fabric will have to be rewoven, for stigmatization is an aspect of social control, and destigmatization implicates loss of social control for the dominant population (G. Becker and Arnold, 1986, 40). If, on the other hand, the cultural and political power structure is to be maintained, stigmatized others cannot genuinely be assimilated into our group and become truly one of "us." In that case, diversity is shown to be a sham.

A related cautionary lesson can be found here for public relations practitioners. Programs developed to address today's stigmatized groups might not be relevant in the next decade and surely will do more to encourage the piecemeal emergence of different stigmatized groups than to solve the systemic problem of stigmatized difference.

Diversity as Variation

Fortunately, the term *diversity* has another meaning, that of variety or multiformity. In this sense, diversity means something more like the proliferation of subtypes of one overarching group, maintaining commonalities while recognizing dissimilarities. Healthy communities are human ecologies comprised of many varieties of the species, each of which contributes some indispensable element to the community and is interdependent with the others. This sense of "variety" is key to reframing diversity as a positive term. One beneficial aspect to viewing diversity as variety is found in Karl Weick's idea of requisite variety in organizations. Weick (1979) argues from a sociotechnical systems perspective that organizations are better able to be responsive to changing environmental conditions to the degree that they have diverse inputs and internal diversity for interpreting and acting on those inputs. The "excellence in public relations project" points out the value of this perspective on diversity (L. Grunig, J. Grunig and Ehling 1992).

From this point of view, diversity among populations occurs naturally because not all persons exist in the same environments within the overall human ecology. By conceiving of diversity as *the normal human condition of variation*, rather than as the recognition of stigmatized differences, at least three main benefits accrue to public relations practitioners, as well as to communication theorists and researchers. First, the dominant population—the one usually not considered to be among the deviant groups—can more readily be seen as equally susceptible to adaptation and transformation in intergroup settings. Basically, "under a presumption of equal worth," as Charles Taylor (1992, 72) says, commonalities among groups can be emphasized in efforts to improve intergroup understanding, rather than emphasizing differences. Second, any population (which has distinctive ways of experiencing and understanding with respect to a particular issue, practice or social context) can be accorded cultural status. As will be seen in Chapter 2 and beyond, this expansive approach will turn out to be an advantage for public relations communicators. And third, efforts to improve intergroup understanding can be refocused on the interactional contexts within which individuals' and groups' needs become relevant. Diversity creates the problematic context of intergroup communication, but variety also provides the means for finding solutions that enrich the whole social ecology.

With this approach to reframing diversity, the core concept of this book—cultural diversity—can be understood as *the normal human variation in the systems of meaning by which groups understand and enact their everyday lives and which they acquire through experiential apprenticeship*. The relevance of cultural diversity depends profoundly on the context of interaction: The critical context where we want to examine the relevance of this variation is the practice of public relations communication. Like the concepts just discussed, however, the term *public relations* is not without its problems and therefore merits a brief discussion.

Defining Public Relations

By all accounts, public relations, both as an academic specialty and as a collection of institutional practices, is a field in search of conceptual consensus and legitimacy (L. Grunig 1992a; Mickey 1997).[5] While there is little agreement on a precise definition of the field, most textbook definitions that go beyond clichés and slogans include explicitly or implicitly as key terms *communication, organization, publics, management, goals,* and *system* (for a more complete analysis, see J. C. Gordon 1997; Hutton 1999). James Grunig and Todd Hunt (1984) coined perhaps the most widely recognized and most succinct definition for the practice of public relations: "The management of communications between an organization and its publics." This broad definition for the field conveys the idea that public relations is goal oriented and strategic, and it is systematically linked with other units in its institution. Public relations also has a mediating and translating role in the communication activities of a society, and it legitimates the expectation that some communication will be two-way. As such, this definition suggests we should conceptualize public relations with a view to including the social consequences of its practice—the constitution of communities of interest.

Profoundly extending this communitarian aspect of public relations, Kruckeberg and Stark (1988) advance the view that public relations is uniquely positioned in contemporary society to restore and maintain the sense of community that was lost with the advent of mass media and high-speed transportation. Their argument is that public relations can be used to re-create community, but only if practitioners enact the role of communication facilitators with a primary goal of altruistic community support, instead of enacting the role of institutional advocate with a primary goal of enhancing the institution's reputation and gaining assent.

While I wholeheartedly endorse Kruckeberg and Stark's communitarian impulse and their critique of the conventional ways of defining public relations's role in society, more can be done with their germinal ideas. Many authorities have argued persuasively that communication is not just action with the potential to create or maintain community, but rather is constitutive of social life (Putnam 1983; Trujillo 1987). In this view, all communication (regardless of its intended personal or institutional purposes) by its social nature contributes in some way to the content of communities, whether inclusive and supportive or oppositional and divisive. The problem for public relations is that the notion of institutional advocacy is intrinsically part of its self-definition and process. Consequently, Kruckeberg and Stark's communitarian ideal for the field better describes processes in which religious, social service or civic organizations could be expected to engage, but not business, industry or governmental organizations.

On the other hand, if Kruckeberg and Stark's idea is modified by recognizing that all communications from all institutions in fact constitute forms of community (both desirable and undesirable), then the objection to their communitarian purpose can be overcome. By this I mean that organizations must recognize that their long-term ability to survive depends on fostering an attitude of social responsibility that nurtures socially healthy communities among their various publics. This observation, by which organizations see their well-being as intimately bound to the well-being of their publics, is not obvious in the short term; over long periods of time, however, the convergence of interests between institutions and their stakeholder publics is unavoidable, and communities—whether positive and supportive or negative and debilitating—are created and maintained. The fundamental goal for public relations, then, is to communicate in ways that nurture the development of positive and supportive communities, communities of which their institutions see themselves as members. At the same time, public relations must recognize the complexity and fragility of communities as well as the limits of inclusion any community can bear: Ronald C. Arnett writes that communicating to build community requires an honest admission "that a community cannot include everything; it is defined as much by exclusion as by inclusion" (1997, 38–41).

Summary

Multicultural public relations can be defined as the management of formal communication between organizations and their relevant publics to create and maintain communities of interest and action that favor the organization, taking full account of the normal human variation in the systems of meaning by which groups understand and enact their everyday lives. Culture is defined and bounded by the subjective experience of communities of persons who share an understanding that some important aspect of their lives differentiates them from other groups. Diversity is a way of referring to the varieties of populations that are on the scene at any given time. What comprises diversity is certain to change over time and across locations.

What is important to remember about public relations in this context is that formal communication in organizations unavoidably creates communities, but those communities are not necessarily desirable for the institution. The task for public relations is to advocate positive community building through effective communication. Just how the phrase *effective communication* can be understood and integrated with public relations practice is the topic of the next chapter.

Notes

1. Reviews of cross-cultural and intercultural communication research literature are included in Gudykunst 1987; Gudykunst and Nishida 1989; Jandt 1998; Kikoski and Kikoski 1996; Limaye and Victor 1991; Lustig and Koester 1999; Wiseman 1995.
2. Diane Alverio, interview by author, Boston, Massachusetts, 19 October 1998.
3. Current demographic data and projections can be found at numerous Web sites gathered at [*http://www.popcon.org//*]; see especially [*http://www.census.gov/population/projections/nation*] and [*http://www.stats.bls.gov/ecopro.table1.htm*].
4. For social-psychological approaches to theories of self- and group identity, see Tajfel 1978, 1982; a sociolinguistic perspective is provided by Gumperz (1982). The foundation for a theory of communication cultures is established in William Labov's (1972) classic work on social aspects of dialect variation. The classic study on stigma is Goffman 1963; also see Katz 1981; Schur 1980; and Ainlay, G. Becker and Coleman 1986.
5. See also Kruckeberg and Stark 1988, 81–82. Scholars continue the search for models and formulas that adequately describe the practices and training requirements of public relations (e.g., Broom, Casey and Ritchey 1997; J.﹒C. Gordon 1997; Hutton 1999; Toth and Heath 1992; see also works on the PRSA body of knowledge project, such as McElreath and Blamphin 1994).

CHAPTER 2

A Theory for Multicultural Public Relations

> Culture is communication and communication is culture.
> —Edward T. Hall, *The Silent Language*

"There is nothing so practical as a good theory." This observation by the psychologist Kurt Lewin implies that theory and action are intimately linked. Steven Corman (1995) demonstrates that almost all human activities are grounded in theories, and he argues that better theories produce improved practices. Educators, professional practitioners and researchers strongly agree that the practice of public relations should be based on well-developed theories (Botan 1993).

When we start out to develop a theory for multicultural public relations, three key questions will quickly come to mind. First, how does the nature of public relations as practiced influence (and possibly modify) our existing theories of intercultural communication? In other words, why do we need a special communication theory for multicultural public relations? Second, given the perspectives on culture, diversity and public relations developed in Chapter 1, what would constitute an adequate theory of intercultural communication? And third, by what standards should we measure the effectiveness of public relations communication in culturally diverse settings?

The purpose of this chapter is to respond to these three questions. First, through a discussion of the nature of communication in public relations, I present an argument for developing a *social-interpretive* theory of intercultural communication that is especially suited for the profession. Then I outline a set of propositions for such a theory, establishing the framework for all later discussion in this book of public relations functions and settings. Finally, based on the theory developed in this chapter and a discussion of communicative competence, I identify a limited number of broadly applicable standards for judging the effectiveness of communicating in multicultural public relations. This approach to effectiveness in multicultural public relations is expanded in Chapter 6, when I discuss the international context.

The Need for Theory

A theory is an idea about how something works, which usually also means how something should be done. Practice is the doing of that something. Thus we have theories about thermostats (Corman 1995), theories about romantic relationships (Berscheid and Walster 1978) and theories about intercultural communication (Ting-Toomey 1994). When we turn the thermostat up or down, when we engage in romantic behavior or when we interact with someone from another culture, we are guided by ideas about how those processes work and what we are supposed to do.

Not to have theories is to act randomly. Until the 1980s, public relations practice was bereft of theoretical foundations (Pavlik 1987), and much of the activity within the profession appeared to be ad hoc and randomly motivated. Since the early 1980s, a simple version of systems theory has dominated the field (Toth 1992; see, e.g., J. Grunig 1992); more recently other theoretical perspectives have been championed, especially rhetorical theories (Botan and Hazelton 1989; Cheney and Dionisopoulos 1989; Toth and Heath 1992). Germinal discussion on interactionism and public relations communication (J. C. Gordon 1997; Mickey 1995) and on postmodernism is beginning to appear (Mickey 1997). To date, however, virtually no work has been done by public relations scholars that develops theory specifically for communication in multicultural contexts.

Intercultural communication, on the other hand, has a strong (though not very diverse) tradition of theory building stretching over at least the past two and a half decades (Kim 1988; Wiseman 1995). While much of established intercultural communication theory can contribute to greater understanding of multicultural public relations, the convergence of intercultural communication theory and multicultural public relations has not been attempted (but see Vasquez and Taylor 1999, for an application of a variable-analytic perspective on culture to the U.S. practice of public relations). Instead of reviewing all intercultural communication theory to identify where it might be applicable to public relations and where it is deficient, I will take a more expedient approach to joining the two fields. In what follows, I discuss the unique communication conditions of multicultural public relations and argue that the nature of public relations raises special concerns for intercultural communication theory.

The Nature of Public Relations Communication

In Chapter 1, culture was conceived as a system of meanings that members of groups acquire through experiential apprenticeship. The diverse systems of meanings and the patterns of communication in which those meanings are positioned are what make a population identifiable and relevantly different from another population. Public relations was presented as the management of communication between an institution and its publics for the purpose of nurturing positive and mutually supportive communities. Public relations is conducted in settings of multiple systems of meaning, systems that are at least partially incompatible.

Within this contextual framework, five characteristics of public relations communication can be identified that help guide the development of a suitable intercultural theory: Public relations is *institutional, representational, ideological, integrational* and *cultural.* Each of these five characteristics emphasizes particular communication conditions and points out what an adequate intercultural communication theory must embrace.

Institutional Aspects of Communication

Public relations speaks not for individuals but for groups of people who are mobilized around a particular perspective on an issue (Grunig and Hunt 1984, 6). George Cheney (1992, 170) argues that "public relations is in the business of producing symbols of, by, and for organizations." The obvious exception—marketing publicity for individual celebrities (such as media stars, athletes and authors)—in many ways treats the celebrity as an economic institution with corporate goals, production functions and business plans. Celebrity publicity aside, in nearly all cases the ostensive function of public relations is to communicate with identified audiences to enhance an organization's image, reputation and relationship with those targeted publics (McElreath 1993; Cheney and Vibbert 1987). Arguing for a rhetorical perspective on public relations, Robert L. Heath (1993, 141) states that theorists "must account for how organizations acquire images, express personae, receive and supply information, make value judgment . . . and advocate as well as yield to constraint. . . . These issues have powerful implications for the identities, identifications, and evaluative perspectives used by persons who work in organizations, conduct business with them . . . [and] judge and regulate them."

Organizational values, goals and actions displayed and spoken about in public relations communication thus are the result of group processes. Organizations' values and goals derive from complex political histories of discussion and decision making (Spicer 1997). Highly strategic and carefully planned actions, which typify public relations activities, often are the result of long periods of consensus building. Accordingly, public relations communication originates in group processes and conveys the rationale for the organization's actions—it is the voice of the organization speaking publicly.

This institutional origin of public relations communication and its function as the public speaker of an organization suggest an important lesson for developing our communication theory. The dyadic, interpersonal focus that dominates current intercultural communication theory must be expanded to include group processes and outcomes at the organizational level. Our theory must be general enough for its propositions to apply equally to personal rhetoric and to "corporate rhetoric" (Cheney 1992).

Representational Aspects of Communication

The identity and voices of an institution are different from those of any individual within it. Corporate persons (the organization referred to as an individual) speak with an impersonal, collective authority. The corporate voice defines itself and rhetorically creates its own character as a separate and distinct organizational person: "Budweiser says know when to say when." But as George Cheney (1992) points out, the corporate person is not like any other natural person in the organization; it is more powerfully persuasive, more abstract and more protected from personal interrogation.

The corporate person is articulated by public relations practitioners. Cheney (1992, 178) notes: "Corporate communication specialists, such as public relations officers, necessarily play an important part in the [corporate message-making] process. They build corporate images that function rhetorically in the appropriation of identity, both individual and collective." Erving Goffman's (1981) idea of *participation frameworks* can be used to describe the role of public relations in creating the corporate person. Goffman posited three possible positions a person might take in any communicative exchange: *principal, author* and *animator*. While Goffman was concerned specifically with face-to-face interaction, his idea can be applied equally to corporate communication contexts. The *principal* is the entity whose values and position on the issue are established in the communication, the person "whose beliefs have been told" (1981, 144). *Author* refers to the entity who created the content of the communication—the speechwriter, copywriter or creator of other official texts. *Animator* is the person who physically performs the communicative act. Deborah Schiffrin (1990, 242) adds to this scheme the idea of *figure*: The character created within the text—the subject whose image is constructed in the communication—is the figure. The corporate person is the source of the values and strategic intention in the message; thus, the corporate person is the principal. The figure is the audience's perception of that corporate entity and is often referred to as the corporate *persona*, which I will discuss later.

In many instances, the same speaker simultaneously has all four participation frameworks. At other times, such as when a chief executive officer delivers a speech written by public relations staff, the CEO is animator and might be principal but often is not author. At least in part, every animator is also figure, because audiences make judgments about performers of communication based on their observations of the performances, and the identities of corporate communicators inevitably are linked to the organizations they represent.

Thus, when Defense Department spokesman Pete Williams (now an NBC newscaster) presented press briefings during the Gulf War, he sometimes participated as animator and author, especially when responding to questions from the press corps; in very large part, though, he spoke for the U.S. Department of Defense, whose positions on reporting the war were worked out in detail by groups of policy-makers.

In public relations communication, then, the principal—that entity whose beliefs are being told in any communication—is the institution in whose employ the public relations communicator labors. The values, policies, problem solutions and accounts for actions are necessarily those of the corporate person, rather than the public relations practitioner personally, although they might be perfectly congruent. A convincing performance by Pete Williams would have left his audiences believing that he spoke *as* the Defense Department, by creating through his performance a personal figure—the persona—whose identity was that of the institution.

In this sense, all public relations communication is representational. Intercultural communication theory must be able to accommodate this "speaking for" nature of interaction: The values expressed, the stories told, even the threshold decision to engage in communication in the first place—all possible motives and means of communicating must be analyzable so that they *could be* those of individuals other than the speaker or writer.

Ideological Aspects of Communication

Ideology commonly is identified as the pervasive power of a group to condition our beliefs and assumptions about the nature of social life (Eisenberg and Goodall 1997, 162). Stewart R. Clegg (1989) identifies two perspectives on this power relationship: In the Marxist tradition, ideology is an effect of positional power, in which the hierarchy of class and authority positions creates a social order of power distribution. On the other hand, poststructuralist theorists tend to see ideology as a set of communicative practices, in which powerful messages about what is natural and right are hidden in the structure and performance of interaction.

I use *ideology* in this second sense. When we say that public relations communication is ideological, we acknowledge that public relations participates in a set of communicative practices that involve subtle messages about what is true, normal and just. Pamela J. Creedon (1993) calls the basic values and norms that an institution relies on when responding to environmental changes its *infrasystem*, and she argues that public relations communication includes institutional infrasystems as an unseen dimension of its messages.

Whenever a public relations communicator attempts to influence a relevant public—that is, whenever she or he officially communicates—the values, goals and preferred images of the institution are being articulated, as well as cues that convey how society should be understood. It is those aspects of communication that are taken for granted (or too subtle for audiences to notice or too culturally "normal" to catch audiences' critical attention) that constitute the ideological. The choice of vocabulary for naming things, the choice of active or passive voice or the way agency is conveyed, the choice of pronouns, the visual images employed—all these are tactics, intentional or not, for inscribing ideological messages in our communication.[1]

An example of public relations communication whose ideology is not apparent is the presentation of women's sports as a unique and independent activity, while it remains in fact a subordinated element wrapped within the metaphors and societal framework of male images of sport (Creedon 1993). Another widely analyzed example is the press conferences during the Persian Gulf War in which U.S. military actions were characterized as just, necessary and successful in large part because of technological superiority. Substantial evidence hidden behind the rhetorical flourishes and dramatic video footage argues for a different interpretation, one in which targeting mistakes, technological failures, diplomatic provocation and bungling, and overestimates of weapons' effectiveness occurred (Jensen 1992; Kellner 1992).

Of course, ideological communication does not have to be misleading or erroneous; it simply expresses and subtly advocates the values and goals of its institution. What is important about the ideological nature of public relations, however, is that some preferred interpretation of social relationships and identities of participants is woven into the very fabric of every public relations communication. Intercultural communication theory must include this ideological aspect of multicultural public relations.

Integrational Aspects of Communication

All public relations communication seeks to build consensus and community among relevant publics. In developing their evolutionary model of public relations from the publicity era through modern two-way symmetrical communication, James Grunig and Todd Hunt (1984) portray the contemporary practice as one of mutual information exchange and accommodation. The fundamental aim of public relations communicators, says McElreath (1993), is to build socially responsible relationships that are at the same time favorable to the organization. Thus, while building a sense of community and mutual understanding, public relations communicators also always have strategic organizational purposes in mind. As such, public relations communication integrates narrow organizational goals with the broader social objective of building productive communities in which various publics—and the organization—conduct their everyday lives.

Accordingly, both strategic organizational goals and social responsibility motivate each communication effort in multicultural public relations. Truly effective public relations achieves the objectives of the organization while it strengthens community relations and enhances the qualities of life within the society it influences (Spicer 1997, 22). Intercultural communication theory needs to address the multiple purposes of institutional communication and the ways those purposes are integrated.

Cultural Aspects of Communication

There are two senses in which public relations is cultural—first, that it communicates across cultural borders, and second, that it is a cultural practice itself. In the first sense, public relations always speaks to audiences who have some point of view in common, a shared understanding that differentiates them from other groups and is often different from that of the public relations professional's organization. Collier and Thomas (1988) argue that contact between populations that hold distinctive perspectives is always intercultural. The central element that makes the populations cultural is their distinctive self-identities.

The most obvious cases of distinctive group identity in public relations communication involve racial, age or gender differences. More subtly, whenever practitioners identify relevant publics, people are aggregated into groups on the basis of their perspectives on and communication about an issue: How aware they are of an issue, how relevant they perceive it to be to themselves, how they interact about it, and what control they believe they have over changing the issue—all these factors bind persons together and affect their status as an identifiable public (J. Grunig and Hunt 1984). Target audiences thus are groups of people who share systems of meaning about particular issues; in other words, they share ways of interpreting and contextualizing the issues of concern. In this inclusive sense, all relevant publics are cultural groups, and public relations communication efforts can be viewed as attempts at intercultural communication.

Second, the practice of public relations is itself a cultural activity. Donal Carbaugh (1990, 7) theorizes communication as "the creation and affirmation of cultural identities in social situations." All communication in this view has a cultural purpose. What makes public relations, in particular, cultural is that it proposes identities of both the organizations it speaks for and the audiences it addresses, and it does so in distinctive ways. Robert Heath (1992) argues that public relations creates the organization's *persona*, its "voice" and "personality," usually in an identifiable speaker. Moreover, public relations communication, Heath says, proposes to audiences ways to think of themselves, ways that will make them better adapted to the organization's persuasive messages. This *second persona* represents a congruence between audience and source, "one that fosters the ends of the public relations effort" (42). Insofar as it depends on audience members' sense of identity, the communion of organization and audience goes beyond just mutual understanding; ideally, public relations communication establishes a joint identity for both. An example of a performance of second persona that experienced problems occurred when U.S. trade representative Charlene Barshefsky testified before the Senate Banking Committee on the U.S. relationship with China. Committee chairman Sen. Phil Gramm asked Barshefsky why negotiations over China's entry into the World Trade Organization were taking so long to conclude. Barshefsky paused and then replied, "What happened, as I said to my staff, is that men never ask for directions, and we mistakenly bombed the Chinese Embassy in Belgrade." With this narrative

Barshefsky effectively established joint identity with her interlocutors but put her organization's persona at risk: This characterization of the executive branch reportedly caused some consternation in the White House and among experts in a U.S. intelligence agency ("CIA's gaffe" 1999). Barshefsky's gendered response played well with an audience of male senators but failed to represent her institutional principal—ironically also a male culture—in a desired way.

Public relations also is cultural because it is practiced within a context of beliefs about public communication. Here are some of the major cultural assumptions of public relations:

- Organizations are social units with rights to communicate publicly.
- Gaining assent through persuasive means is preferable to using coercive means.
- The mobilization of public sentiment is not only possible but can constitute a threat or benefit to organizations.
- Institutions have public images that can be modified by communication activities.
- Society is always communicated with in segments, as targeted special-interest publics.
- A corporate person can be substituted for an individual as the responsible agent for decisions.

These premises are not typical nor often dominant in noncapitalist societies or in other arenas of communication. For example, the very idea of public opinion as an important force for institutions to reckon with was inconceivable in the former Soviet Union (Matveyev 1991). The fact that public relations is made possible by the credibility of a largely independent and competitive press is irrelevant in societies where news coverage is controlled by central government authorities.

These cultural aspects of public relations communication indicate that intercultural communication theory must be sensitive to both interaction that creates and displays identities among cultural groups and communication as a culturally coded system of expressing identity. It must concern itself with the content of interaction as well as the cultural resources and assumptions of communicating in any particular instance.

In summary, the nature of public relations tells us that an adequate theory of intercultural communication must account for: (1) the institutional sources of messages; (2) the speaker as representative of the institutional source; (3) the ideological aspects of communication; (4) the tension between organizational strategic goals and motives that are grounded in social responsibility; and (5) the nature of public relations communication as a cultural practice involving the formation of identities and assumptions about the nature of communicative practices.

A Social-Interpretive Communication Theory

In recent years numerous authors have noted the emergence of an alternative orientation to the scientific tradition in communication theory. This alternative view is variously called the interpretive perspective, the new paradigm, the postpositivist view or social approaches (Denzin 1997; Leeds-Hurwitz 1992; Penman 1992; Putnam 1983). I will refer to this perspective as the *social-interpretive* view. It embraces many ideas and systems of thought emanating from philosophy, linguistics, sociology, anthropology and critical studies of literature; however, most descriptions of the social-interpretive view have in common a few basic and important assumptions about social life, knowledge and action.

The scientific tradition views social reality as objective, as governed by natural laws and rules capable of being discovered through appropriate scientific techniques and as predictable and (ultimately) controllable by people. In contrast, the social-interpretive view holds that what passes for social reality is constructed by people in communicative interaction: What is important about social reality is the meanings people assign to it. Social-interpretivists are interested in how the meaning-construction process is experienced by people and the relationship between those meaningful experiences and social structure.

Theory in the traditional perspective isolates units of social life and, treating units as variables, establishes statements that link those units. As Young Yun Kim (1988, 16) describes it, in the social scientific tradition,

> theory is commonly viewed as a set of principles, often called axioms or laws, that are taken as "nomothetic" [lawlike] statements, from which a set of probabilistic statements, called propositions or theorems, are derived. In this tradition, causality is essentially one-way and linear, and prediction (and thus control of outcome) is its most desirable goal.

On the other hand, the goal of theory in the social-interpretive perspective is to develop general statements about the nature of reality and of knowledge and human action and then from those concepts derive descriptive propositions about specific communication phenomena of interest. In what follows, I identify five assumptions—the general conceptual statements about reality, knowledge and action—that frame a set of theoretical propositions describing (and prescribing) communication in multicultural public relations.

Theoretical Assumptions

First, any social action is based in part on voluntary motives and decisions. Since humans are creative beings, communicative action is not wholly mechanistic nor based on predictable responses to environmental stimuli. This assumption of voluntarism means that theorists and researchers cannot expect to discover a natural law that exhaustively explains communicative behavior, and our observations as researchers always will have limited generalizability (Penman 1992, 236). It means also that prediction is a weak function of theory and is secondary to the more central functions of description and explanation of observed natural events and settings.

Voluntarism also means that communication is grounded in values. Robyn Penman (1992) points out that if theory and research (and professional practice, too) are not objective processes of discovery and management but are in part human inventions, "then all research [and other practice] is also value based" (239). Her point is that communicative practices have a moral dimension because they have a base in human choice making. What pass for knowledge and action based on our knowledge are in part "of our own making," and we are responsible for creating what is desirable or undesirable and for many of the consequences of communication. It is in this sense that all communication is value based; there is no purely objective and values-free research or other professional practice. Thus, some communicative actions are better than others, given the contexts of interaction, and the question becomes one of deciding what standards will identify better research and communication.

The second assumption of the social-interpretive view is that reality is socially constructed. By this theorists mean that the ways humans understand phenomena—the meanings constituting relationships, actions and objects—and what is accepted as knowledge are products of human interaction in historically embedded contexts. If meanings are created and re-created in human interaction, then meanings are relational and fluid, subject to constant change. It also implies that knowledge is always tentative, continuously under revision and conditioned by the politics of personal and institutional power.

The third assumption is that knowing and sensibly acting are made possible only by the use of symbolic codes. Codes are systematically organized sets of signals that cultural groups use for eliciting meaning and assigning meaning to phenomena. Languages are the most obvious symbolic codes, but groups also use systems of gestures, dress, dance, chants, rituals and so forth. Because being human means to use culturally conditioned codes to understand the world and relations within it, culture is central to a social-interpretive theory of communication.

Fourth, theorists, researchers and practitioners cannot remove themselves from the social process they are studying or managing. Theory changes the world by proposing an understanding of it; research findings are used as part of our base of knowledge upon which we conduct our everyday lives; and managing a professional activity like public relations is not to stand outside relationships between organizations and publics but to constitute those relationships. In short, the social-interpretive perspective holds that theorists are framed by the same contexts as those persons and processes they are trying to explain.

The fifth assumption of the social-interpretive perspective is that all communicative action has implications for self- and group identities. Communication always conveys both explicit information about a topic and information that proposes a definition of the participants and their relationship (Watzlawick, Beavin and Jackson 1967). A hotel employee relations manager, for example, tells new workers in their first employee orientation meeting important information about hotel policies and employment benefits. Her way of conveying that information, however—her tone of voice, vocabulary, facial expressions and choice of media—signal to the new workers that they are subordinate to her, less powerful and highly dependent on her, and are still outsiders (Banks 1988, 26–27). As Wendy Leeds-Hurwitz (1992, 134) points out, "The psychological view of the self is replaced by a more appropriate cultural, socially constructed view of the self." Identity thus is not a fixed attribute of a person but a multifaceted aspect of interaction that undergoes continual modification.

These five assumptions—human voluntarism, the social construction of reality and knowledge, the centrality of symbolic codes and culture, the subjective nature of research and practice and the importance of identity—comprise a set of foundational ideas from which propositions about communicating in multicultural public relations can be derived.

Theoretical Propositions

Propositions are general statements of what can be expected of participants in specific communication situations. Propositions thus are descriptive state-

Table 2.1   Propositions of the Social-Interpretive Theory for Communication in Multicultural Public Relations

---

Proposition 1: Public relations communicators are understood by their relevant publics as strategic agents.

Proposition 2: Public relations communication is interpreted within the cultural contexts of recipients, not sources.

Proposition 3: All public relations communication proposes identities of participants.

Proposition 4: Social and personal assessment of values in public relations communication is culturally conditioned.

Proposition 5: Public relations communicators are identified as representatives of institutional interests.

Proposition 6: Public relations communications are understood as candidate versions of reality.

Proposition 7: Public relations communication reflexively creates those social communities within which its institution must operate.

Proposition 8: Public relations practitioners are responsible for the ideological content of their communication.

---

ments of applied principles, moving from the broad concepts articulated in assumptions "to more specific theories of communication activities or phenomena" (Carbaugh and Hastings 1992, 160). As such, they are statements of probability characterizing what is expectable, and they are linked to assumptions by the notion of the usual and the habitual. Propositions of the social-interpretive theory for multicultural public relations are shown in Table 2.1.

Proposition 1: Public relations communicators are understood by their relevant publics as strategic agents. The assumption of voluntarism says that communicators always "could have done otherwise." Thus, communicators are seen by audience members as capable of choosing from among a range of communicative options. The meanings imputed to public relations communication will be based on a habitual conclusion that the sources of public relations messages have chosen their content, media and contexts intentionally. Accordingly, the responsibility for those imputed meanings will be placed on the public relations communicators rather than on audience members themselves.

Proposition 2: Public relations communication is interpreted within the cultural contexts of recipients, not sources. While taking the cultural perspective of the other is often cited as an important intercultural communication skill (e.g., Gudykunst 1991, 121), public relations audiences cannot be ex-

pected automatically and always to take the cultural perspectives of the practitioner. This is true partly because members of relevant publics are the parties being appealed to, while the public relations practitioner is the party
seeking to change the other's knowledge, attitudes or behavior. More criti-
cally, public relations audiences are multiple and diverse, while the source of
a public relations message is typically unitary and institutional. Therefore,
the choice of symbolic codes that are culturally meaningful to publics is the
responsibility of the public relations practitioner.

*Proposition 3: All public relations communication proposes identities for
participants.* Identity commonly refers to the multifaceted sense of self-iden-
tification derived from one's personal experiences. Most interpretive theorists hold that people maintain a wide array of personal, social and cultural
identities, which are subject to modification in interaction and are treated
as a cohesive autobiography. Ting-Toomey (1993, 73) argues that despite
some stable continuity in one's generalized identity, "each communication
episode produces an inevitable change in this mosaic sense of self-identifi-
cation." For example, while you might identify yourself as a woman, you
also might identify yourself as an educated and experienced lobbyist, as an
African-American, as a parent, or as a Catholic.

*Proposition 4: Social and personal assessment of values in public relations
communication is culturally conditioned.* When meaning is assigned to communicative behavior, an inevitable part of the meaning is the assignment of
relevance, truth, utility, goodness and other assessments of value. This is so
for two reasons. First, all communication is achieved by the use of cultural
codes. Second, culturally encoded signals are always interpreted within a culturally textured setting, the practical setting in which the recipient must
make decisions of preference in order to survive and prosper.

*Proposition 5: Public relations communicators are identified as representa-
tives of institutional interests.* By its functional nature, public relations is
a form of intergroup communication whose messages express a collective
viewpoint. Public relations practitioners thus communicate not as individuals but as institutional representatives, and members of relevant publics in
turn communicate with them as if interacting with those institutional interests.

*Proposition 6: Public relations communications are understood as candi-
date versions of reality.* Narrative theorists using an interpretive perspective
view the reality experienced by individuals as story texts (Arnett 1997;
Mumby 1993). Concerning any issue, numerous stories are proffered as arguments for what reality is, and the story accepted as the true story is likely
to be the one that individuals find resonates with their prior experience and

is internally coherent (Fisher 1987). Consequently, public relations communications will be accepted as reflecting reality only if they harmonize with the cultural experience of audiences.

Proposition 7: Public relations communication reflexively creates those social communities within which its institution must operate. With each interaction between public relations practitioners and relevant publics, the relationships are redefined; whether the levels of trust, support and cooperation are confirmed or changed, the world is not the same as before the interaction. In an incremental way, public relations influences the social fabric of the network of relationships in which it exists.

Proposition 8: Public relations practitioners are responsible for the ideological content of their communication. Since ideology is inscribed "beneath the surface" of communication in its structure and the subtle details of language and images, it is not readily detectable by participants. More important, recipients of public relations communication interpret its content within their own cultural frames of reference; it is a rare cultural perspective that places a high priority on detecting ideological elements. The worldview of institutions and their perspectives on power relationships are encoded by institutional communicators—intentionally or not, consciously or not. The ideological consequences for audiences are thus the responsibility of public relations practitioners.

These eight propositions unfortunately do not give communicators standards for effective communication. To develop those guidelines, it is necessary to clearly state what effectiveness is and how it is to be fostered.[2]

Intercultural Communication Effectiveness

To say what is effective communication is to identify a principle of acceptability or preference. Traditional views of effectiveness are derived from the idea of the competent communicator, assuming that effective communication can be identified by analyzing the skills, goals and knowledge attributed to speakers and writers (Spitzberg 1983; Ting-Toomey 1993, 72).[3] Gudykunst (1991, 1993), for example, argues that effectiveness in intercultural communication means the degree to which interactants are able to avoid misunderstanding. As "one of the major factors involved in our perceptions of competence," he states, effectiveness "is related closely to the notions of adequacy and sufficiency" (1991, 101). Competence in this view is an attributed quality based on a communicator's motivations, skills and knowledge.

The traditional perspective on intercultural communication broadly sees effectiveness as qualities persons have that are applied across situations and across time. The social-interpretive view, on the other hand, avoids any deterministic definition of effectiveness, so that the assumptions of voluntarism and the social construction of reality can be maintained. Instead, a social-interpretive notion of effectiveness focuses on the contexts in which communication occurs (more specifically, the contexts in which receivers make sense of others' messages) and the nature of interaction itself. Borrowing from Collier and Thomas's (1988) cultural identity approach, I view effectiveness as *the successful negotiation of mutual meanings that result in positive outcomes* in any communicative activity. Positive outcomes are, minimally, reinforcement of participants' self-concepts, affirmation of cultural identities, enhancement of the relationship and accomplishment of strategic goals.

These four criteria can be combined with Penman's (1992) ideas of "good communication practice" to establish guidelines for effective multicultural public relations communication. Penman says good practice involves a recognition that communication constitutes social relationships and knowledge, rather than just being a tool for informing or changing people. In addition, good communication recognizes that people create meanings in particular contexts of time and place, and their interpretations of communicative actions will inevitably be diverse. Finally, Penman argues that events always are open to new interpretations, that meanings are never final and fixed.

Effectiveness in multicultural public relations, then, is assessed by the degree to which communication:

1. reinforces participants' self-concepts;
2. affirms participants' cultural identities;
3. enhances the parties' relationship;
4. accomplishes the parties' strategic goals;
5. embraces the constitutive nature of communication;
6. recognizes the contextual nature of meanings;
7. accepts the diversity of interpretations; and
8. remains open to reinterpretation.

This chapter has established criteria for judging effectiveness in multicultural public relations communication. The standards are based on a theory of intercultural communication derived from the functions of public relations practice and the assumptions of the social-interpretive perspective on communication. Its central constructs are meaning, identity, culture, ideology and contexts.

With these standards of effectiveness in mind, and relying on the theoretic propositions that describe the social-interpretive view of public relations communication, we can now turn to analyses of specific relationships where multicultural public relations occurs.

Notes

1. For further discussion of the ideological nature of communication, see Deetz 1992; Fairclough 1989; Fowler et al. 1979; Kress and Hodge 1979; Mey 1985; Mumby 1988, 1993.
2. *Effectiveness* as I am using the term here is not related to the sense of public relations effectiveness alluded to in the IABC "excellence in public relations" project. In that work, effectiveness is variously construed in terms of practical utility and adherence to prescribed norms of practice, and it is loosely related to a derivative concept of organizational excellence (see J. Grunig 1992; Dozier, L. Grunig and J. Grunig 1995). Closely allied with this approach to effectiveness is the project on measuring and evaluating public relations effectiveness sponsored by the Institute for Public Relations Research and Education (see Lindemann 1997).
3. Martin (1989), Spitzberg and Cupach (1984, 1989) and Wiseman and Koester (1993) provide a wide variety of studies of interpersonal and intercultural communication competence.

CHAPTER 3

Communicating with Multicultural Internal Publics

> Communication technique shapes the form and the internal economy of organization.
>
> —Chester I. Barnard, *The Functions of the Executive*

For nearly all organizations, one of the most important publics to communicate with is the organizational members themselves. Wilcox, Ault and Agee, for example, call an organization's employees "a crucial audience for its public relations department" (1995, 361). That is so because organizing is nothing if not coordinated collective action; hence, nothing productive gets done without some form of members' assent to harmonize their goals and activities. To a great extent, orchestrating members' activities must be achieved through communication.

Despite the synchronizing effects of task coordination, though, it is a mistake for organizational communicators to treat members as if they were all the same. As I argued in Chapter 1, not only is cultural diversity within the work force inevitable, but it enriches the creative material available to organizational leaders, making for a healthier organizational ecology. As an example of diversity enriching the organization's ecology, consider the case of an urban hospital I worked with. For years the medical center had experienced chronic turnover and high absenteeism, especially among the nursing service and housekeeping department employees. Large numbers of workers who were single parents, many with preschool children, chronically struggled to meet conflicting demands of their jobs and their home lives. On the job they saw themselves as an interest group with qualities in common that affected their views about many work activities and decisions; however, their voices were not recognized by top administrators as a legitimate public. When the medical center management hired a consultant to survey the attitudes and needs of the workers, the consultant translated to management a strong desire in the work force for help in resolving the problems of single workers with child-care responsibilities. A task force comprised mainly of single-parent employees from various occupations and managerial positions created a program that combined on-site facilities, some paid child-care workers and strong employee volunteer participation to provide home chore and child-care services. The nominal program costs to the medical center were more than offset by reduced turnover and improved attendance. The single parents remained as an interest group, in some cases helping other employee populations innovate social programs that had bottom-line accountability while providing needed employee services.

This example shows how it can be in the best interests of top management and public relations communicators to recognize and respond to multicultural internal publics. Creating such responses within a social-interpretive view of multicultural public relations is the subject of this chapter. First, I explore the nature and scope of internal publics. Next, I join the debate about valuing diversity versus managing diversity, arguing that these are not mutually exclusive perspectives and can be included in a social-interpretive approach to effective communication. In addition, the communication theory for multicultural public relations is applied to the most critical functional areas of internal public relations. Finally, these areas are identified by examining major public relations textbooks (i.e., Baskin, Aronoff and Lattimore 1997; Cutlip, Center and Broom 2000; Grunig and Hunt 1984; Seitel 1998) and practitioner literature on employee communication. These functional areas involve building multicultural teams, making and communicating decisions (including health and safety communication), managing conflict episodes and recognizing diversity in rewarding performance.

The Nature and Scope of Internal Publics

Several of the more popular textbooks do not present separate units about internal publics (McElreath 1993; Newsome, Turk and Kruckeberg 2000; Wilcox, Ault and Agee 1995). This omission is noteworthy because the absence of a special focus on employees and other internal publics indicates that some educators might believe internal publics can be treated theoretically the same as other, external publics. The mere fact of members' economic dependence on the organization argues otherwise. In addition, the complex personal relationships, functional interdependencies, authority hierarchy and need to establish convergent goals and activities make internal publics quite unlike other audiences.

Some educators have argued that internal publics include all persons who "share the institutional identity" (e.g., Newsome, Scott and Turk 1993, 140–42). This definition, however, founders on the shoals of deciding what the "institutional identity" is and how, to what degree and by what mechanisms persons share that identity. Thomas Becker and Robert Billings's (1993) research on organizational commitment demonstrates that substantial numbers of employees in many organizations do not identify with their organizations at all. Many professionals identify with and have a primary allegiance to their occupation or social unit outside the place of employment.

Moreover, from the social-interpretive perspective, an institutional identity can not be objectively observed, counted and differentiated from other identities. Certainly leaders try to foster positive worker identification with the organization and develop goals and values all members share.[1] Yet research has shown that cultural groups vary considerably in their achievement goals and work values (Holt and Keats 1992). In addition, with diverse cultural populations in a work force, it is impossible for an organization to create an institutional identity that is consistent with all members' personal identities. Communicators therefore must be mindful of both the more stable, personal aspects of self-identity and the aspects that reflect group memberships—both work groups and cultural groups—as well as the subjective nature of identities.

For our purposes, *internal publics are all persons who provide substantive work within the organization,* either for pay or as volunteers, regardless of their occupational or authority positions. Under the umbrella of internal publics will appear a wide variety of populations with diverse interests and traits in common: Some will be obvious and easy to identify, such as race- or gender-based groups; some will be subtle and will require sensitivity to their efforts to identify themselves as a group with cultural interests, such as single parents or the deaf (Dolnick 1993). Barbara Walker makes the important observation that race and gender can be taken as metaphors that refer to all differences: "This reference is based on the discernment that, whatever the difference, the dynamics of the conflict or struggle created by discomfort with differences are the same" (1991, 14).

I prefer a more general metaphor based on music. Nearly 20 years ago, my colleague Penelope Trudeau and I helped develop work teams in VA hospitals by using the example of a symphony orchestra. In a training film we used, Zubin Mehta explained that bringing the instrumental sections of the orchestra together to perform as an effective whole requires blending the unique creative contributions of each instrument while orchestrating the interpretation of the music. The musical metaphor is even more apt today, as new genres of music are invented, exotic instruments are imported from around the world and unprecedented experiments in musical forms are tried.

Valuing, Managing and Communicating

Two basic approaches to the issue of engaging diversity have become established in recent years, and they have been contrasted within the "valuing versus managing" controversy (Geber 1990; Stewart 1993; Thomas 1992). Some human resources practitioners advocate the "valuing differences" model developed by Barbara Walker when she directed the diversity project at Digital Equipment Corporation in the 1980s (Walker 1991; Walker and Hanson 1992). This approach recognizes that the range of differences among people that systematically can obstruct individuals' effectiveness— the range of differences "that make a difference"—is infinite. The valuing-differences model typically focuses on awareness, attitude changes and self-empowerment. In small-group settings, employees from various levels and jobs identify their own stereotypes and attempt to "strip them away." Next, people are encouraged to build relationships with those they see as different from themselves. The third phase builds on these relationships by emphasizing self-empowerment through appreciating and even trying out others' ideas and values. Finally, group differences are probed to achieve a better understanding; this activity "is an important step toward developing effective strategies to help people learn how to work together interdependently" (Walker 1991, 12).

At its core, valuing differences is an individual-level effort to change attitudes and values. It assumes that interpersonal work done in small groups across a work force can significantly alter the fabric of relationships and enhance individuals' quality of working life, which in turn indirectly will improve productivity. While it might be true that harmonious relationships will improve productivity in cases where differences between individuals have resulted in chronic, intractable conflict, research on employee satisfaction shows that, in the absence of serious obstacles, highly satisfied employees are not necessarily more productive than employees of average satisfaction (Euske and Roberts 1987, 45; Eisenberg and Goodall 1997, 200). Moreover, there is little evidence that changing workers' awareness of individual differences will result in changed behaviors on the job, even if there is substantial change in attitudes toward differences (Thomas 1991). The precise mechanism by which empowerment is generated also is not addressed in Walker's model.

The strongest criticisms of the valuing-differences view are made by advocates of "managing diversity" (e.g., Carr-Ruffino 1996; Thomas 1991, 1992, 1996). Thomas's argument is that the valuing-differences model is too concerned with individual-level change while failing to emphasize organizational goals and functions as the focus of diversity programs. The managing-diversity perspective, as Lea Stewart (1993, 3) points out, "emphasizes work output, not necessarily the means used to obtain that work." Organizational needs and bottom-line consequences are the yardsticks by which diversity activities are measured, and managing diversity is expected to occur at individual, work group and total organizational levels of interaction.

Loden and Rosener (1991) argue that valuing diversity is a corporate philosophy about personal values, while managing diversity is a practical skill aimed at changing organizations' culture (see also Harris and Moran 1996). It is an organizational development effort whose central problematic is intergroup prejudice. While it is clear that what organizational members choose to do about diversity can have an impact on an organization—even if it is simply to modify dominant attitudes and values about differences— the central issue from a social-interpretive perspective on multicultural public relations is communication effectiveness. That is, communication that affirms participants' identities and relationships while fostering achievement of their respective goals is the action most needed in multicultural work settings. As such, the social-interpretive view subsumes projects to enhance the understanding of differences as well as efforts to improve organizations' performance through reducing intergroup prejudices. Table 3.1 represents a comparison of the three perspectives on diversity in internal publics.

The steps that can help organizational members learn to conduct effective multicultural communication involve aspects of both the valuing-differences and managing-diversity models. Those steps are explained in Chapter 8; however, they can be summarized here as follows:

1. Establish awareness of cultural groups and an accurate understanding of relevant differences.
2. Recognize identity issues and communication needs.
3. Practice mindful communication behaviors.
4. Implement cultural mindfulness in public relations communication.
5. Evaluate communication effectiveness.

More about the concept of mindfulness (Langer 1989) can be found in Chapter 8. Also relevant to effective multicultural internal communication is the concept of genuine dialogue, which is explained more fully in Chapter 4. These procedures, taken together, open the way for public relations

Table 3.1   Comparison of Valuing-Differences, Managing-Diversity
and Social-Interpretive Models

	Valuing-Differences Model	Managing-Diversity Model	Social-Interpretive Model
Nature of Model	corporate philosophy	managerial skills	communicative action
Type of Diversity	individual, subjectively defined	individual and group, defined by management	group, consensually self-designated
Focal Problem	stereotyping	prejudice	meanings
Explicit Goal	individual empowerment	organizational development	effective communication

practitioners to engage in multicultural communication with any relevant
public. The sections that follow highlight the conditions of specific communication functions involving internal publics—in building multicultural teams, making and communicating decisions, managing conflict episodes
and recognizing diversity in rewarding performance.

Building Multicultural Teams

Socialization is the process of making individuals into organizational members; as such, it is the core of team building. Critical socializing functions
are communicated throughout the span of each employee's working life, and
they involve almost all official communication, from policy directives and
newcomer training to incentive awards and disciplinary discussions. The
bulk of organizational communication research identifies three situations or
activities involving higher levels of management where socialization as a focused communication activity takes place: (1) at organizational entry and
other career transition points, (2) in supervisor-subordinate interaction and
(3) in formal training activities.

Organizational Entry

What members believed about an organization before crossing the threshold for the first time is called anticipatory socialization (Jablin 1985). Members' expectations of the organization are influenced by their vocational so-

cialization, by job information received in the job search process and by cultural learning. Much of this information is the result of organizations' public relations communication efforts that address other audiences, such as communities, media and educational institutions. Thus, organizational entry is a point in the communication relationship between organization and member where employee relations and other functions of public relations converge. This convergence tells us that it is not possible to communicate with employees in a totally controlled and unitary program: Communication with external audiences can affect the nature of the communication relationship with internal publics. Perhaps more important, Jablin (1985, 693) states that anticipatory socialization results in inaccurate newcomer expectations of both job and organization, which "will make the organizational assimilation process more difficult for the newcomer."

The organization's basic objectives in newcomer socialization are threefold. First, socializing agents convey information about task achievement (e.g., how the job is done here), positional relationships (e.g., who to see about a certain kind of problem), employment conditions and benefits (e.g., how much sick leave can be accrued) and procedural rules (e.g., how to properly request and use sick leave). Second, established members instruct newcomers in the informal ways of developing and maintaining good relationships; that is, they communicate about how personal communication is done around here. And third, agents instill appreciation for the organization as an institution and foster understanding of the core values and ideas on which the organizational leaders base policies.

Newcomers' goals typically mirror those of the organization: to obtain information about the job, working conditions and benefits; to learn the work rules and administrative procedures; and to understand relationships and the rationale for the organization's policies. Newcomers also place their sense of self-identity under stress because of the foreignness of the organizational setting (Van Maanen 1977). At no other time is the individual's identity more challenged than at organizational entry. Although scholars have pointed out that each new member is a challenge to the organization's status quo, it clearly is the newcomer who is under pressure to change if she or he is in some way different from the rest of the membership. Loden and Rosener (1991, 49) report research showing that newcomers who are seen as more different are subject to more severe testing and hazing by organizational members. Similarly, at critical points of career transition—such as promotion, retraining or organizational exit—workers' self- and group identities are disturbed by the disruption of roles, relationships and work routines. Consequently, communicators must take special care to address identity issues and to affirm individuals' cultural identities during socialization communication.

Supervisor-Subordinate Interaction

A member's communicative relationship with his or her supervisor is critical not only to successful adjustment during organizational entry, but also throughout the employee's career. Jablin (1985, 699) summarizes relevant research in this way: "Findings of studies consistently indicate a newcomer's relationship with his or her initial supervisor can have long-term consequences on the success of the individual's organizational and professional career." Moreover, the supervisor-subordinate relationship remains critical to worker satisfaction (Hatfield and Huseman 1982) and effectiveness (Eisenberg and Goodall 1997) throughout an individual's working life.

Despite the importance of the supervisor-subordinate relationship, severe gaps exist between supervisors and subordinates in their understanding of such organizational issues as job duties, decision authorities and the nature of communication in organizational relationships (Jablin 1979). In addition, it often is the case that neither supervisor nor subordinate recognizes the degree to which they misunderstand one another (Smircich and Chesser 1981). Such gaps in understanding can influence task achievement, decision making and employee satisfaction, and can be made worse by cultural differences that block or distort communication (Stewart 1985).

Gail Fairhurst and Theresa Chandler have studied in-group and out-group communication in supervisor-subordinate relationships (1989). In-group communication displays high trust, high levels of mutual influence and support and the use of both formal and informal rewards; out-group communication relies more on formal authority and shows low trust, low support and low use of rewards. In-group communication is associated with improved performance, higher satisfaction, lower employee turnover and smaller gaps in understanding.

Both closing the gaps in understanding and fostering in-group perspectives on relationships depend centrally on effective communication. In multicultural settings, being open and supportive is necessary but not sufficient supervisor behavior. In addition, these goals require sensitivity to differences in language and the need for expert translation (Banks and Banks 1992), an understanding of cultural norms regarding hierarchical relationships, use of a flexible and adaptable interactional style, and strategies that promote the positive self-image of others.

Training Activities

The same competencies and practices are also needed in training contexts. Employee training efforts—whether designed to improve task skills, inform about program changes or modify attitudes or values—are attempts to dislodge individuals' ways of doing things or seeing their world and instill new ways of doing or seeing. As such, training is an attempt to alter ways of being in the workplace and thus demands that persons' self-identities change.

To meet all eight criteria for effectiveness in multicultural public relations as described at the end of the previous chapter, two additional caveats are appropriate for the training context. First, trainers must anticipate cultural resistance to traditional training techniques and formats. Some populations learn more effectively through stories, dramas or visual images than through lectures, logical exercises and demonstrations. Two ways of determining the most effective training procedures for specific populations are to consult relevant research literature and to ask members of the population for their views. Relatedly, Loden and Rosener (1991, 212–13) emphasize the value of tutoring and coaching as alternatives to traditional training and mentoring programs.

The second caveat is that the content of training programs—and the rationale for the training—should be provisional and thus subject to revision. In his research on empowering organizations, Michael Pacanowsky (1988) has identified six rules that foster member empowerment. Among Pacanowsky's rules are the requirements to promote full, open and decentralized communication; to broadly distribute power and opportunities; and to practice challenges to established routines and assumptions within an atmosphere of trust. These qualities must be carried over to training encounters, because training has a profound influence on member knowledge, values and identity, and it is an activity where organizational leaders most directly seek to influence members. When training content is left open to reinterpretation and revision, Pacanowsky says, the organization can "become wise" by learning from unexpected sources.

To sum up so far, public relations communicators have a fundamental role in member socialization and training, and effective multicultural communication means that they should:

1. guard against hazing and testing newcomers of diverse populations;
2. pay special attention to identity issues during organizational entry and career transitions;

3. remain aware of language differences and provide expert translation, as well as alternate media and channels;

4. prepare supervisors to be sensitive to cultural differences in all interactions;

5. design and implement job training that is not dogmatic and is open to new interpretations and ideas; and

6. provide broad-based learning opportunities and distribution of strategic information.

Making and Communicating Decisions

With the rise of the human relations and human resources traditions in organizational theory, workers' roles in decision making became a focal concern of both managers and scholars. Human relations theory recognized the importance of individuals' social needs and desire for control over aspects of their own working life; human resources scholars advocated authentic efforts to enrich jobs and the genuine participation of members in decisions that could affect them in their jobs. Today, however, decision making by work groups is a routine matter, not just because participation is good for workers' morale but also because organizations have seen real gains in productivity, quality and innovation as a result of group decision making.

Most researchers recognize that group decision making is a demanding interpersonal process that often shows stages of development and cyclical phases of interaction. B. Aubrey Fisher (1980), for example, held that decision groups experience four stages: orientation, conflict, emergence and reinforcement. In the orientation stage, members of a group clarify their task and explore the nature of the group, including learning about one another's assumptions and positions. The conflict and emergence stages involve advocating positions more forcefully, bargaining, forming coalitions and eventually achieving consensus on solutions. Reinforcement refers to the period after a decision has been announced by a group, when members experience a sense of mutual accomplishment and solidarity. Each of these stages is made more taxing if some members are seen as stigmatized by difference.

Although some researchers have found no consistent pattern of group processes of decision making, most groups experience some periods of disorganization, periods of examining basic assumptions and individual and group motives and periods of work on the group's interaction (Fisher 1980; Hirokawa and Rost 1992). Thus, group decision making occurs frequently, is profoundly communication oriented and often involves exploration and debate on the nature of members. In these circumstances, a social-interpretive view of multicultural communication sensitizes participants to the need for eliciting and valuing perspectives and experiences from all group members and for treating decisions as unfinished business—as discussions that are subject to revision.

Certainly the quality of employees' participation in group decision making can affect organizational outcomes. Public relations communicators typically would be more concerned, however, with the influence of cultural diversity on the process of informing internal publics about decisions already made by organizational leaders. Critical to this communication context are the credibility of the source of messages, the sensitivity of sources to workers' cultural identities and assumptions, and communicators' skill at framing policies and decisions in ways that are truly informative to diverse populations.

Source credibility can be enhanced by relationships that are trusting, open and authentic. Frank recognition and valuing of differences is a prerequisite for members of organizations to trust and communicate openly (Walker 1991). Similarly, knowing the values, assumptions and identity issues of diverse populations is necessary for sensitive communication of any sort. Thus, genuinely open dialogue built around exploring and valuing differences is a prerequisite to effectively communicating decisions to a diverse work force.

Managing Conflict Episodes

Conflict is normal and ubiquitous; without conflict, social relationships stagnate or decline (Wilmot and Hocker 1998). Thus, while Americans nearly always think of conflict in negative terms, it is part of inescapable and potentially beneficial processes in organizations (Ting-Toomey 1985). Conflict occurs when parties in an interdependent relationship with scarce resources perceive that the other is interfering with a desired goal; hence, conflict is relational. More often than not, the real conflict is about the nature of the parties' relationship, rather than about a content issue, although conflict often disguises itself as being about an objective problem. Conflict encounters are opportunities for people to choose between competitive, exploitative behaviors aimed at acquiring a finite resource and collaborative, creative behaviors aimed at mutually solving problems. Regardless of which choice of strategy parties make, conflict management and resolution are cultural processes (Ting-Toomey 1994).

Because conflict is cultural, diverse populations differ in their approaches to conflict. Nadler, Nadler and Broome's (1985) cultural model of conflict management identifies three ways that people differ culturally in their views on conflict. First, groups differ in their *basic orientations* toward the value of conflict (positive versus negative), toward the manner in which conflict is resolved (degrees of assertiveness and cooperativeness) and toward the degree of finality in resolving conflict episodes. Second, cultural populations differ in their *personal beliefs* about how fairness, trust and the use of power are related to conflict. Third, groups differ in their *message strategies* and range of *conflict styles*.

These conflict factors provide a basis for developing guidelines for the public relations communicator, whether as participant in a conflict relationship or as a third party trying to resolve others' conflicts. Recognition that parties to a conflict can hold vastly different basic assumptions about the purposes, benefits and procedures for engaging in conflict is essential to effective conflict communication. Moreover, as Cushman and King (1985) argue, the differences in approaches to conflict between groups' cultural norms and the organization's culture can further block effective conflict communication. Once again, as in socialization and decision making, it is necessary to first address the issues of difference before getting into the substantive content of the conflict.

In addition to applying the aforementioned principles for socialization and supervisor-subordinate interaction, the principles of social justice can be applied to promote effective communication in multicultural conflict situations. Jerald Greenberg and his associates have conducted research for more than a decade on organizational justice (e.g., Greenberg 1987, 1990, 1993). Greenberg has developed a taxonomy based on four dimensions of justice—procedural versus distributive and structural versus social (see Figure 3.1). The structural dimension of justice involves environmental contexts of organizational life, so that what is of concern is ensuring fairness in the application of rules. The social dimension is concerned with the interpersonal treatment of members and the equitability of reason giving and information. Procedural justice refers to the content of procedures, while distributive justice is concerned with the fairness of outcome distributions.

From this set of dimensions, four types of justice can be identified: *systemic justice,* or fairness in procedural rules; *configural justice,* or fairness in the distribution of resources and rewards, including positions and explicit authorities; *informational justice,* or fairness in providing members information about procedures so they can know the reasons for procedures and accounts for how they have been used; and *interpersonal justice,* or fairness in accounts for specific actions taken and their consequences.

Greenberg (1993) points out that the latter two types of justice—the

Category of Justice

		Procedural	Distributive
	Structural	Systemic justice	Configural justice
Focal Determinant			
	Social	Informational justice	Interpersonal justice

Figure 3.1 A taxonomy of justice classes.

two based on social dimensions of justice—are often overlooked in programs to achieve a fair and just workplace, yet they contribute significantly
to reductions in conflict and workers' negative attitudes toward unfavorable
events. In one study, for example, Greenberg (1993) found workers' negative reactions to a smoking ban at work were lower if they were given full
information and justification for the policy; additional reduction in the negative feelings was achieved if the communication showed high sensitivity to
the difficulty of refraining from or quitting smoking.

The lesson from justice research for public relations communicators is
that intercultural conflict in the workplace can be mitigated by going beyond structural justice strategies to focus on the communication of informational and interpersonal justice. Providing full and frank justifications for
policies and procedures while communicating concern for the identity needs
of diverse populations and in-group solidarity can build a community of
trust and collaboration rather than distrust and antagonism.

Recognizing Diversity
in Rewarding Performance

A key aspect of organizational distributive justice involves the system of rewards. Fairness says that persons will be rewarded according to their contributions to the organization (equity based), according to the way others who
are similarly situated are rewarded (equality) or according to individual need.
Although the tradition in the U.S. workplace has been to establish distrib-

utive justice by rewarding alike people who are in like jobs and and have like tenure (equality basis), a dramatic trend favors rewarding on the basis of equity (Boyett and Conn 1991; James 1993). Different values and concepts of justice are served by each of these reward systems. Equality-based rewards reflect a system that values harmony and cohesiveness; equity-based rewards are oriented toward productivity and competition. Keith James (1993, 24) notes that "even in profit making U.S. corporations, when egalitarianism, harmony, and relationship maintenance come to be the major goals, equality allocation principles and democratic, participative, negotiative procedures are likely to be used."

These factors present organizational communicators with an apparent dilemma: To emphasize productivity, an organization needs to use equity rewards; yet to emphasize harmonious relationships, an equality reward system seems better. Edward Lawler (1993, 10–11) argues that "new approaches to management must be based upon employee commitment and employee involvement rather than upon top-down control," and reward systems must be based on "the business objectives of the organization and the kind of culture, climate, and behaviors that are needed for the organization to be effective."

Thus, organizational values and core principles need to be identified as foundations for structuring reward systems. Lawler points out that a central function for communicators is to manage beliefs and perceptions about rewards: "The perceptions and beliefs that individuals develop are partly a product of the practices and behaviors of the organization, but they are also influenced by the statements that an organization makes—or fails to make—about its values and intentions" (1993, 38). Identifying core principles and values and then effectively communicating them to members are preludes to creating a "total compensation mix." The complete reward package will vary from organization to organization but can include both equity and equality rewards across the entire work force or by subunits, effectively resolving the dilemma of choosing between the two.

In line with the concepts of informational and interpersonal justice, it also is vitally important that reward systems be explained, justified and applied effectively. Here is a key role for public relations communicators—the communication of organizational values, core principles, the procedures and rationale for reward systems and the reasons for actual distributions of rewards. Ceremonies and special awards for recognition of member contributions must be designed with social justice in mind. To do so effectively with multicultural publics, members' beliefs and values about the following elements should be surveyed and procedures build around the results:

- the nature and benefits of competition
- the desirability of public recognition for achievement
- the desirability of material and intangible rewards
- the desirability of advancement and authority
- the desirability of equity or equality rewards
- the benefits of commitment to organization, to individuals and to family or other outsiders
- the desirability of performance feedback

These recommendations for effectiveness in rewards—communicating core principles and values, informing about the procedures and rationale for rewards, devising mechanisms for giving special recognition and justifying the distribution of compensation and awards—assume that the organization's values and structures embrace multicultural membership in the first place. Only when the values underlying effective multicultural communication are made core elements in the routine life of the organization will the recommendations here take root.

Communicating effectively with multicultural internal publics is a highly complex task of boundary management. Boundaries are the zones of separation between individuals, groups and entire organizations, and they demark differences that can be perceptual, emotional, interactional or physical, or combinations of these. Susan C. Schneider (1991) argues that boundaries in organizational relationships are where differentiation and integration get negotiated. While strong boundaries promote increased in-group autonomy and control, they also reduce integration and harmony. Schneider states the problem this way: "A crucial dilemma faced by organizations is how to maximize a sense of identity and autonomy in individuals and groups, yet maintain the necessary interdependence and integration as well as efficiency" (185).

Her solutions to maximizing both autonomy and coordination contain elements of the valuing-differences and managing-diversity approaches as well as the social-interpretation view. Leaders should differentiate and clarify functional boundaries, while foregrounding individual and unit interdependencies and empowering individuals by helping them learn how to negotiate boundaries. In addition, Schneider recommends focusing on organizational goals, while enabling "interdisciplinary teams to perform required tasks without unnecessary adherence to ideology or professional/functional loyalties" (1991, 186).

All these responsibilities affecting internal relations—managing diversity, building teams, generating decisions, managing conflict, distributing rewards and conducting boundary maintenance—are more demanding at the beginning of the 21st century than ever before. The pace of environmental and social change requiring organizational adjustments is occurring at unprecedented rates. Organizations are adopting new communication and information-management technologies and in the process are transforming themselves repeatedly. Such changes are placing ever greater stress on organizational members and their relationships. While these trends are discussed in detail in Chapter 6, I should emphasize here that technology is not a complete solution to problems of increased demands for productivity and adaptability. At best, technological fixes can provide process innovations and economies in production and distribution; it appears, however, that they do not significantly help form more stable interpersonal relationships and communities of stakeholder publics and organizations.

The recommendations for public relations communicators in this chapter contribute to building organizational communities that are both diverse and cohesive, communities where diversity is both valued and managed in an ongoing exploration of ways to live together productively. In the next chapter, many of these principles are applied to interaction between organizations and external communities.

Note

1. George Cheney has contributed much to the theory of organizational identification. See Cheney 1983a, 1983b, 1991; Tompkins and Cheney 1985.

CHAPTER 4

Multicultural Community Relations

Any kind of community is more than a set of customs, behaviors, or attitudes about other people. A community is also a collective identity; it is a way of saying who "we" are.

—Richard Sennett, *The Fall of Public Man*

The continual use of strategic communication will widen the chasm between opposing people and their ideologies.

—Ronald Arnett, *Communication and Community:*
Implications of Martin Buber's Dialogue

The terms *community, diversity, identity,* and *dialogue* already have appeared or figured prominently in this book. In this chapter, I use these concepts to develop a new approach to effective communication in multicultural community relations. This is a "new" approach because taking a social-interpretive view of the communicative relationship between institutions and their external publics calls for a more flexible and multilayered sense of community than most public relations scholars and practitioners conceive of it.

Following an exploration of the nature of community relations, I develop the idea that any institution's communities are multiple, complex and internally diverse. Perhaps the most important idea in this chapter, however, is the final section's discussion of dialogue. Dialogue is both the defining principle and the mechanism for conducting communication relationships within communities.

Varieties of Community Relations

The dominant public relations view of community is the social unit of residents where the organization is located. Baskin, Aronoff and Lattimore, for example, call the community "the folks next door" (1997, 270), and they adopt William Gilbert's definition of community as a "place of interacting social institutions which produce in the residents an attitude and practice of interdependence, cooperation, collaboration and unification" (272). Center and Jackson (1995) refer to this entity as the "home/community"; the Public Relations Society of America defines it as "an organization's geographic operating area." Taking a more subtle view, James Grunig and Todd Hunt (1984) distinguish between community as a locality and publics within a locale who have a community of interest. Still, their notion of community is "rural areas, small towns, urban centers, or neighborhoods or suburban areas within an urban complex" (267) comprising an organization's geographic locality where relevant publics reside.

Along with this popular assumption that community is the place where an organization is situated, some scholars suggest that the concept of community in public relations might be outdated. In an era of global telecommunications, the home office, remote markets and resources, media shopping and transportation systems that permit unprecedented mobility, the concerns of a local neighborhood seem anachronistic. Indeed, Newsome, Turk and Kruckeberg (2000) take an issues-and-functions approach to their analysis of public relations, rather than focus on subspecialty areas by generic type of public. Wilcox, Ault and Agee (1995) organize relevant portions of their text by subspecialty publics, but community relations is not treated as a separate area of application; instead, it is covered as a functional aspect of public affairs. Most representative of this change of view, Cutlip, Center and Broom's seventh edition of their classic textbook (1994) eliminated entirely the chapter on community relations that had been included in previous editions, and it remains absent in the eighth edition of their book as well (Cutlip, Center and Broom 2000).

Community and Social Responsibility

It appears, then, that public relations educators are not comfortable with the concept of community and find it difficult to justify focusing program resources on communication activities with publics defined by their geographic location (see Baskin, Aronoff and Lattimore 1997, 276–77). Yet organizations are becoming more aware of their social responsibility and its impacts on their survivability, and the idea often is linked with locale. Baskin, Aronoff and Lattimore (1997) point to the trends of neighborhood pride and community activism as well as larger-scale social movements, all of which necessitate corporate involvement in their community activities.

Cutlip, Center and Broom (2000, 464) call the 1980s a "new era of corporate social responsibility" and the 1990s and beyond a time of increasing diversity in the public relations roles in corporate good citizenship. With respect to the 1990s and beyond, Patrick Jackson (1993) has asked, "Can community relations be the *core* of PR programming?" And he answers with a firm, "Yes, because it sets the *true* tone of what an organization stands for . . . in the communities where [organizations] conduct business."

Nonetheless, if the community is treated as a locality where the organization operates and its relevant publics are the people who live there, four conceptual problems arise for community relations. First, it is not community as a locale with which public relations people communicate, but representatives of particular publics that reside within that locale, as Grunig and Hunt point out. The particularity of the relevant publics thus will depend on issues, while geography makes the issues salient. In this view, community relations is difficult to differentiate from consumer, government, media, education or investor relations, except on the basis of where those functions are carried out. With this approach to definitions, organizations are forced to conduct communication activities under a false umbrella, and social responsibility is conceived primarily as philanthropy (Cutlip, Center and Broom 2000, 469–73).

Second, by viewing community relations as addressing people residing in our neighborhood, "they," as targets of our communication, are separated from "us." Two-way symmetrical communication becomes incongruous, if not fictional, and one-way communication is favored. Third, a paradox exists in the fact that "we" also often live out there in the locality among "them." Thus, the line between internal communication and community relations also becomes blurred: Can we treat ourselves separately as members of the organization and as members of the community?

Finally, the traditional view of community and community relations invites organizations to see social responsibility as something they give to others whose interests are distinct from their own. When connections are made, it is to link philanthropy with corporate profitability (Conference Board study 1993). The dominant view of community relations discourages organizations from conceiving their enterprise as an organic element of a larger social system.

Against Community Relations

A social-interpretive view can help resolve these difficulties created by structural-functionalist definitions of public relations subspecialty areas. Richard

Sennett (1976, 222) argues that the "garden variety" sense of community as "a neighborhood, a place on the map," is too narrow in today's society, "because people can have all sorts of experiences of community which do not depend on living near one another." Instead, Sennett says, for communicators to avoid treating others as objects—an inherently immoral form of relationship—community must include the sense of revealing one's authentic self to others and establishing a common identity and shared action. Sennett decries that the loss of genuine community as public participation in our culture has diminished to a localized perspective; an antidote to the loss of community is the advancement of common identity and shared action through authentic self-disclosure—in effect, the recognition, building and empowerment of publics.

In a similar vein, Ronald C. Arnett (1986, 16) differentiates association and community: "If the principles of a group are significant, but the relationships are minimized or viewed as irrelevant, then only association, not community, is fostered." Elaborating on this distinction between association and community, Arnett describes the way the theologian and philosopher Martin Buber contrasted the social and the *interhuman*:

> Buber laid out four major differences between the "interhuman" and the "social." First, the "interhuman" realm is a personal relationship in which the individual [or group] is met as a noninterchangeable, nonobjectified contributor to the activity. On the other hand, the "social" realm has the person's function or role as the most significant concern. Second, the "interhuman" is the realm of the "between"; it is not a psychological construct. Meaning is found not in one partner, but "between" partners in interaction. In contrast, in the activity of the "social," meaning is possessed by one party or another. Third, the "interhuman" is grounded in the assumption that what one does is more vital than how one appears. . . . The "social" life switches this emphasis. . . . Finally, the "interhuman" realm invites dialogue by permitting ideas to "unfold" in conversation, unlike the "social" realm, in which one pushes to "impose" a particular perspective prior to hearing the other's views.

Following Buber, Arnett's view of community says all parties to communication are part of the community—community is not a label for others but a way of referring to a relationship that includes the self, the other and a set of communication principles. In addition, Arnett points out that community is a concept that must include conflict, for without differences of views, no change would be possible and the community would lack vitality. As we learned in Chapter 1, diversity benefits a community's ecology because it challenges the status quo and promotes adaptation.

Community relations, then, is the public relations program that enhances a particular kind of relationship with external publics, a relationship that is inclusive, self-revealing, genuine, personal and emergent. In this sense, my argument is against community relations as a subspecialty of the practice of public relations, because all external communications should be conducted within the framework of Buber's idea of community. The same community attitude should apply to investors, customers, suppliers, media representatives and people who live in the organization's neighborhood. Community relations thus should be a description of an attitude toward communicating, rather than a subspecialty or functional area. This perspective defines community relations as the motives and techniques for communicating a sense of community with any relevant external publics.

Cultural Diversity and Community Relations

The social-interpretive view of community relations will be upsetting to many PR practitioners and educators, some of whom would argue that an organization, especially a profit-making corporation, has interests that are incompatible with those of many external publics, and vice versa. The parties who typically matter more than others are organizational leaders, financial stakeholders and customers. Traditionalists also would argue that as an element in an organization's strategic planning, the first and highest obligation of public relations is to enhance the firm's competitive position. As Cutlip, Center and Broom put it, *"Public relations must contribute to achieving the profit goal of business in a competitive environment"* (2000, 460). This means community relations as traditionally conceived militates against those who would take a competitive stance toward the firm, criticize it or inhibit its profitability.

This traditional view is an oversimplification. Corporations (or any other organizations, for that matter) do not operate in splendid isolation from the rest of society, acting only when they determine that their self-interests are at stake. Consider, for instance, Voltex, a fictional name for a company that manufactures batteries, other power sources and power conditioning devices. Besides officers, investors, members and customers, many other individuals and groups have critical interests in the activities and decisions of Voltex. Suppliers of raw materials and transportation companies work for Voltex's continuing success in the marketplace. The U.S. Department of Labor has legitimate interests in Voltex's hiring and work safety practices. The Internal Revenue Service and state and local tax authorities have concerns for the proper accounting practices at Voltex. Neighbors of the half-dozen Voltex plants keep surveillance over how the firm handles and disposes of heavy metals and acids. Hispanic leaders in the city where the new Voltex plant is being built want to be assured that Voltex will make employment opportunities equally available for all local citizens. Golf cart manufacturers need to know about the quality and quantity of Voltex products and the reliability of management commitments. A citizen who does not buy Voltex batteries and lives a thousand miles from any Voltex facility pays her taxes to support a government she expects to effectively regulate the manufacture of batteries. And so on: It is possible to link functionally almost any individual and group with any organization in an interdependent system where social meanings attached to practices are the common ground.

Without mutual identities and shared activities and goals with such entities, Voltex will encounter needless opposition. More important, the mere fact that Voltex extracts sustenance in terms of careers and good will (and typically extracts profits as well) from the social system of which it is part obligates Voltex to avoid privileging some groups over others. It is in Voltex's own long-term interests to communicate so as to promote the inclusion of all individuals and groups who express a relatedness to the organization. In a genuinely inclusive relationship as described in the foregoing paragraph, Voltex can openly advocate its own positions, goals and needs, while working with other members of the same social system to serve their interests.

In addition to these functional relationships between Voltex and the rest of society, the organization has a clear moral connection to the community. Amitai Etzioni (1993) argues that community is the "moral voice" of a social unit, the shared sense of good conduct and reason that binds people and institutions together and reinforces their values. As organizations become increasingly interested in social responsibility, it becomes clearer that they must take account of the needs, moral standards and expectations for good conduct among populations they touch. This attitude of shared responsibility toward community relations is exemplified by the Tom's of Maine personal health products company. Tom's of Maine practices "common good capitalism," a policy of building relationships with publics that "extends beyond product usage to include full and honest dialogue, responsiveness to feedback, and the exchange of information about products and issues" (Common good capitalism 1994).

The varieties of populations an organization might touch not only are numerous, they also are likely to change in short order. As the discussion in Chapter 1 showed, diverse cultural groups arise as issues and concerns crystallize with their identity needs. Multicultural external publics can be found among the media (Does your organization recognize a connection with women's publications?), investors (Have you made contact with an association of African-American entrepreneurs and financiers?), professional organizations (Is it relevant to you to know that gay and lesbian sections of many professional associations lead their groups to hold annual meetings only in states that are receptive to gay and lesbian rights?), consumers (Does it make a difference if your customers are increasingly aware of environmental issues?) and so on.

In addition to being dispersed by functional areas, multicultural external publics also are found across geographical locations. Often widely dispersed corporations fail to reckon with the fact that they have multiple plant sites; more likely, those whose processes are mobile or widely scattered— such as shipping and transportation companies, franchisers, dealerships, partnerships and utilities—sometimes neglect the impact they have on individuals and groups based on personal contact in specific locations. Sometimes it is hard to recognize the connection. The movement of an interstate bus company's service through geographically widespread areas and populations expands the number and types of contacts the firm experiences with others. The relevant community in the traditional sense of locale quickly becomes incalculable.

In addition, many organizations' outputs reach groups of people the organizational leaders never contemplated as publics. A case in point is the Hanford nuclear facility in the state of Washington. For decades Hanford officials paid scant attention to health complaints from residents living remote distances from the nuclear reservation until it was learned that airborne discharges from normal operations and experiments at the facilities moved over vast areas downwind and affected the health of those "downwinders."

In sum, the traditional view of community relations as a program to interact with local leadership is not viable. Problems of defining the community, identifying relevant publics and limiting the domain of issues all argue for an alternative perspective. The social-interpretive view reframes multicultural community relations as a philosophy and method of communication that applies to all external publics, diverse groups of people who will identify themselves as having a relation to the organization but who often can be sought out before grave differences arise. The key characteristics of community relations are:

- *inclusive:* aims to create a sense of "we-ness"
- *revealing:* process based on authentic self-disclosure

- *personal:* others are not objects or targets but stakeholders in the social system
- *multiplex:* levels, locations, populations vary, depending on issues
- *dialogic:* interaction based on dialogue

The social-interpretive view of community notwithstanding, organizations still have their dual public relations obligations to foster their own interests through advocating issues and enhancing image and to be socially responsible. If the community is self-defining and multiplex, what communication techniques can an organization use to achieve these dual obligations? Martin Buber supplies an answer to this question with his concept of *dialogue.*

Community Relations as Genuine Dialogue

Social-interpretivists hold that communication constitutes relationships, and the nature of the communication activity—not just the content but also the intentions and interpretations of participants—conditions the nature of the participants' relationship. In a recursive system, the relationships people believe they have with one another provide context for interaction, while reciprocally each instance of interaction sediments a particular relationship. For a community of the sort just described to develop through communication—a community based on mutual benefit, flexibility in defining social reality, shared goals, authentic disclosure and genuine validation of identities—the form of that communication must be consistent with the desired community. This is not to say the interaction must be the same with all populations; the underlying principles, motives and values must be consistent, but their expression must be diverse, flexible and creatively resourceful because of the diversity among populations.

The underlying principles, motives and values that are necessary for effective community relations are established in dialogue. For Buber (1965), genuine dialogue is one of three forms of communication. *Monologue* is discourse that expresses an institutional role, disguises the source's intentions and identity and seeks only self-confirmation. *Technical dialogue* is discourse that asserts facts to inform or persuade audiences. Both monologue and technical dialogue involve what Buber (1965, 22–23) calls *reflexion,* conceiving the other solely in relation to one's own needs and experience as a type or stereotype, and a refusal to grasp the other as a unique individual "in his particularity." "In short," Arnett (1986, 7) concludes, "self-centered conversation is monologue. Information-centered conversation that assumes neutrality is technical dialogue. Relationship-centered communication that is sensitive to what happens to both self and other approaches genuine dialogue."

Genuine dialogue begins with turning toward the other. It occurs in a social space between the participants Buber calls "the narrow ridge," which defines not similarity or mutuality but a zone of openness where genuine identities are displayed and positions on issues are negotiated. Communicating on the narrow ridge means offering to the other party both an authentic display of who you are and what you stand for and a receptivity to the other's authenticity. It means striving to meet on the common ground of the narrow ridge, to find commonality and to agree to strive jointly in pursuit of mutuality.

Complete mutuality, Buber (1965, 178–79) argues, is beyond human practical ability: Each party must remain faithful to the structural requirements of the relationship (such as teacher-student, therapist-patient, producer-consumer, borrower-lender, etc.), or else there might be no basis for their contact in the first place. On the other hand, dialogue is not intended to capture a psychological condition of participants in communication; it is a process that by definition brings out something new between participants, invites the creation of a text that would not exist but for the genuine openness of the parties.

In multicultural public relations, the requirements for engaging in genuine dialogue are captured in the social-interpretive perspective on communication. As populations show themselves to be relevantly connected to an organization, an engagement must occur that has at least the following characteristics:

- full and genuine disclosure of identities, positions on issues and concerns, strategic intentions and relevant values
- balancing attachments to prior definitions of issues and positions with a sincere openness to alternative versions of reality and positions
- striving for mutual solutions to problems and mutual definitions of the common good
- genuine efforts to validate the other's identity through culture-sensitive communication

Culture-sensitive communication involves, first, a recognition that the other is an interpreter of the text created in dialogue. This means that each party must fashion contributions to the dialogue with the other's worldview and interpretive resources in mind. For Buber, to be human is to use language, and to speak to another in genuine dialogue is to speak as that person would, in forms of language that create a social bond with the other.

Steven Kepnes (1992) notes the relationship between Buber's ideas on language and dialogue and those of the Russian literary theorist and linguist Mikhail Bakhtin. Bakhtin recognized the social constitution of language and the communicative constitution of society. His theory of dialogue includes a sense of the term that refers to an opening up of creative possibilities between participants. This openness toward the other and toward the issue between them means that neither party controls future events: "Nothing conclusive has yet taken place in the world, the ultimate word of the world and about the world has not yet been spoken, the world is open and free" (Bakhtin 1984, 166).

Dialogue thus means also to give up control over issues and others' responses to and actions on issues. In this way, genuine dialogue as the activity component of community relations can empower multicultural publics, providing an opportunity to create definitions of issues, the nature of interaction with institutions and the solutions to problems institutions pursue.

But what are the particulars? How are public relations communicators to "do" dialogue? The dialogic approach to community relations can be viewed as four responsibilities in creating and maintaining effective relationships among diverse publics: outreach, leadership, conflict management and relationship maintenance.

Dialogic Outreach

Outreach means to search for and to learn to recognize individuals and populations who might have a stake in the organization. This responsibility includes looking beyond the organization's neighborhood to areas where people might be impacted by the outputs of the organization, like the "Downwinders" of southeast Washington, northwest Oregon and north Idaho. It includes seeking out in regions the organization affects persons and groups unlike ourselves and those who might not appear to have concerns about the organization—the impoverished and homeless, recent immigrants, aboriginals, academics or any others who are not among the usual publics. It also includes providing mechanisms for others to freely initiate contact with the organization. Such simple mechanisms as toll-free telephone and Internet-based communication services for providing fast, personal contact with human representatives of the organization would be a start. Maximizing opportunities for face-to-face interaction, as I advocate in

Chapter 6, should be a guiding principle. Finally, Buber warns that in creating community, it is wise not to be so formal and programmatic about it—not to talk about the process so much—that others will resist building a relationship for fear of being maneuvered into a persuasive seduction. Building communities based on dialogue takes time, patience and persistence because trust must be built incrementally.

Leadership and Dialogue

Ronald Arnett (1986) offers guidelines for dialogic leadership. First, communicators who are leaders in large organizations must recognize their superior economic power and their ideological force with respect to most publics. To be already in a position of control over resources and institutional processes can tempt leaders into believing they therefore *have* rights to control community decisions; moreover, it can delude leaders into believing they *are* right, right on the issues and in possession of the right vision for the future. Second, leaders must be willing to strive as authentic, recognizable individuals to use persuasion and judgment—rather than manipulation, intimidation or coercion—to move audiences to accept their vision. While not all leaders can be characterized as manipulators or bullies, public relations is widely criticized on the basis of its misleading communication practices. Third, leaders must accept the limits of their own knowledge and vision, leaving open the possibility they will be persuaded to change. And last, leaders "must embrace a long-range perspective that extends beyond immediate recognition by one's fellows and calls the community to a higher level, while simultaneously being open to having that vision tested by counter perspectives" (Arnett 1986, 156).

Dialogue and Conflict Management

Among the basic findings of conflict management, three can be formulated as guidelines for dialogic community relations. Augsburger (1992) demonstrates that conflict is a cultural activity. He points out that personal concepts of conflict are culturally conditioned; as a result, while organizational members might assume that the causes, tactics, resolutions and values involved in conflict are universal, outsiders might maintain quite different ideas about it. Thus, conflict in multicultural relationships often takes place within settings that already have high potential for misunderstandings. Part of dialogue, then, is sensitivity to different interpretations of the nature of conflict, the permissible responses to and expressions of differences, the possible resolutions of conflict, and the nature of values used to ratify conflict. Fairness, for example, among many U.S. populations means equality (the same distribution for each party); among others it means equity (or distribution of outcomes according to parties' relative contributions); in still others it might mean the distribution of outcomes according to each party's needs.

Second, conflict requires multiple parties; consequently, each party contributes to the occurrence of conflict and each must own up to its contribution. Third, conflict is normal and even desirable if change is to take place. We often overlook the profound contributions the minority voice, the dissenter, can make to social change. Arnett (1986, 104) reminds us that "from the narrow ridge perspective, we cannot follow any single position in all instances; if we do, we cease to invite dialogue and begin to prescribe a technique. . . . We cannot at all times permit the majority viewpoint to control the arena of decision making."

And fourth, collaborative approaches to conflict result in more creative solutions and higher satisfaction for the conflict parties than do competitive approaches (Hocker and Wilmot 1995). Alfie Kohn (1986) concludes that "with astonishing regularity [researchers] have found that making one person's success depend on another's failure—which is what competition involves by definition—simply does not make the grade." To collaborate, however, does not mean to cave in. Collaboration includes vigorous defense of interests and ideas in a spirit of upholding the other's identity, dignity and legitimacy. Collaboration means jointly finding the best mutual solutions through civil argumentation.

Dialogic Relationships

The final responsibility of dialogic communicators involves maintaining community-based relationships. While issues and groups will emerge and subside over time, organizational communicators must provide full and honest feedback to others in the community about the implementation of agreements, continue to inform them of possible changes of plans and conditions and keep returning to those publics for help in creating the "moral voice" of the organization.

At the same time, organizational leaders must remain open to initiatives by others to establish relationships. Those initiatives might express approval of the organization, or they might be critical of decisions and operations. In either case, organizations cannot assume others initially will interact in a spirit of genuine dialogue. As I argued in Chapters 1 and 2, the responsibility for setting the tone and moral stance in relationships lies with organizational communicators. By displaying a commitment to genuine dialogue, public relations communicators can instruct others in ways to foster effective community relations.

This chapter has argued that a locality-based concept of community is inadequate. In place of the traditional view, the social-interpretive approach treats community as an array of relationships involving the organization and emergent publics of potentially vast diversity, based on the actual and possible impacts of the organization on others and created by dialogic communication. Dialogue, as Martin Buber conceived it, fulfills the criteria of the social-interpretive view of effective multicultural communication: It validates participants' identities, builds humane relationships and allows for mutual goal achievement while remaining open to reinterpretation and revision. When genuine dialogue occurs, "community is where community happens" (Buber 1965, 31).

CHAPTER 5

Communicating with Multicultural Activists

> The most progressive managers . . . will move away from a focus on structure and toward a focus on values, away from the notions of control and domination and toward participation and involvement, away from rule-bound conformity and toward a sense of community, away from a preoccupation with the internal and toward a better understanding of those outside, away from rigidity and toward adaptability, and away from a pretension of value-neutrality and toward high standards of ethics and morality.
>
> —Robert T. Denhardt, *The Pursuit of Significance*

As described in Chapter 4, community relations is effective when an organization reaches out to create genuine dialogue with diverse groups of people who might be affected by the organization. Activist communication, the subject of this chapter, is the inverse case: Organizational decision makers establish receptivity to genuine dialogue following initiatives by self-designating groups whose actions are intended to change the organization.

In many cases, the external activist groups are homogeneous. But the very fact of their activism indicates that they will be culturally different from organizations they have concerns about: They perceive events and interpret their meanings differently, and they rally around a unifying need not acknowledged by the organization. Thus, they have a sense of identity distinct from that of the organization. In many other cases, activist groups are internally multicultural, because they are coalitions of cultural groups with a focal interest in something the organization has done, is rumored to have done, or is planning to do. For these reasons, it is rare that public relations practitioners engage in dialogue with external activist groups who are culturally similar to organizational decision makers.

This chapter examines from a social-interpretive perspective who might be encountered as activist groups, what the typical contexts of activism are, and how best to establish genuine dialogue with activists. It is important to recognize that activism is not limited to persons and groups outside the organization's presumed boundaries; member coalitions who raise issues to policy-makers also qualify as activists. Many of the principles discussed in Chapter 3 therefore will apply to the discussion of external activists as well.

Within this discussion I will challenge conventional views of crisis communication and two principles of public relations that have achieved the status of sacred rules—the wisdom of being proactive and the "one clear voice" maxim. Occasionally in this chapter I will use the term *concerns* to mean topics that individuals or groups believe are especially important and require resolution. I use this as a broader term than *issue*, which I will distinguish as one of several types of situational factors that generate activist communication.

The Nature of Activist Publics

Multicultural activists are special "others" since they proclaim themselves as having a community of interest in a concern not identified by the organization as something important but to which the organization must attend. Contrary to popular assumption, the organization does not "create" activists or define them as an audience by public relations strategic communication. This has been a central idea of activist communication, because nearly every public relations textbook identifies the process of *doing* public relations as one of defining the problem (often called issues identification), segmenting publics (which is the same as creating an intended audience), planning and executing a communication campaign and evaluating the effort.

This formulaic approach to what public relations practitioners do when communicating with activists is expressed in John Marston's (1963, 91) RACE acronym (research, action [i.e., planning and programming], communication and evaluation) and in Center and Jackson's (1995, 14–15) four-step "proactive" public relations process of (1) fact-finding, (2) planning and programming, (3) action and communication and (4) evaluation. Thus, it is assumed that *doing* public relations fundamentally includes setting the scope and nature of the concern and creating audiences for strategic communication. Such is clearly not the case with activist groups. They knock on management's door, usually without invitation and often with the prior involvement of government agencies or the mass media. In this sense, they are conducting public relations campaigns with the objective of changing the organization.

Moreover, activists open interaction about concerns that they, not the organization, initially formulate. For example, Cutlip, Center and Broom

point out that the animal rights movement embodies a social issue not recognized by organizations but with profound consequences for them. Not-
ing that People for the Ethical Treatment of Animals (PETA) has suddenly
grown into a huge movement, these authors argue that "cosmetics manufacturers, medical research laboratories, meat packers, and even federal government agencies have had to factor views of this new activist force into their
decision making" (2000, 228). Because of activism by PETA, many cosmetics firms no longer test their products on animals, and the message "not
tested on animals" has become to many consumers a sign of quality manu-
facturing. PETA activism also influenced the Pentagon decision to discon-
tinue animal-based combat wound research and has brought to light alternative research techniques for university laboratories. Similarly, a group of
environmentalists who also are employees of the National Forest Service
have joined together to bring new perspectives and concerns in forestry to
the attention of agency decision makers (Barker 1993).

Many public relations theorists and practitioners view activists as the
enemy. James E. Grunig and Todd Hunt (1984, 309), for example, call
activist publics "powerful adversaries for most organizations." Philip Lesly
(1992, 326–27) calls them "opposition groups" and likens them to "multiple anarchies" who conduct "insurgence against leadership." E. W. Brody
(1991, 188) refers to activists as "dissidents," and he notes that the Foundation for Public Affairs tracks dissident groups in the publication *Public Interest Profiles*. This portrayal of activist publics conceives of organizational
relationships as comprised of competitors vying for limited resources in a
zero-sum game. If they win, we lose, is the implied logic of the traditional
view.

In contrast, a social-interpretive perspective recognizes that both the organization and what it treats as its environment are socially constructed in
the communicative behavior of members and others. With balanced and
well-informed interaction, organizations and activists can create a synergis-
tic relationship that benefits both parties. On this point, Cheney and Vibbert (1987) describe the history of public relations as one in which the social construction of environments has been misguided and unproductive to
organizations because activists were conceived as the enemy or merely as targets of persuasion campaigns.

Enacted Environments

Only recently have theorists begun to tease out the implications of treating
"the environment" as enacted. According to Karl Weick (1979), organiza-

tions pay attention to some aspects of the chaotic events in the world and ignore others. They attempt to make sense of those events they pay attention to, labeling and characterizing those elements as constituting the world they live in. They then act toward their perceived world, and the consequences of their actions—including many unintended consequences—become elements of the chaotic world to which they must continue paying attention (or disattending) for the purpose of creating order. In this way, organizations contribute much to their own environments and have considerable influence on their fates.

This is not to say that enacted environments are purely imaginary—the death of a customer from taking cyanide-laced Sudafed, as occurred in Washington state in 1992, represents a tragic and irrefutable reality. But Weick's argument does point out three principles that support the social-interpretive view. First, policy-makers choose what is important to attend to, and in doing so they define the reality of their environment. Reciprocally, organizational reality is that which has gained official attention. This accounts for the way institutions can be "blindsided" by an issue or trend, as the U.S. auto industry was in the late 1970s and early 1980s by the issue of product quality and major investment houses were during the late 1990s by the advent of online trading. Second, not only is the environment enacted, but what it means—in terms of intentions, consequences, values, motives and organizational intelligence—also is socially constructed. This implies that organizations, like individuals, act on the basis of negotiated meanings; thus, "environmental scanning" (Anderson 1992) alone is not sufficient for effectiveness. And third, environments are *both* obdurate facts *and* socially constructed interpretations. Some elements of an organization's relevant world impose themselves on the organization and are largely self-defining, such as the immediate impacts of a natural disaster. A consequence of this view of enacted environments is that proper actions—those with the most favorable long-term outcomes for both the organization's stakeholders and society—require a full, open and egalitarian exploration of all concerns raised by any party so as to reach a joint understanding of conditions.

Interactivity and Interdependence

Constructing activists as the enemy is a *reactive* stance; it says, "When they show up we respond to them defensively." Cheney and Vibbert (1987, 172) argue that fundamental changes in the relationships between large corporations and various publics in the 1970s, particularly the big oil companies, fostered *proactivity* through issues management: "These problems faced by the oil companies 'represent' in a useful way the constraints and accommodations that have come to structure contemporary public relations in the corporate setting." These authors call the corporate persuasion of publics "the latest transformation of public relations" (173).

Yet several of the lessons James Post and Patricia Kelley (1988) derived from their interviews and extensive review of the public relations issues management literature focus on *interactivity*. Post and Kelley note that "the desire to be proactive has been tempered by the realization that 'interaction' is more appropriate to the type of interdependence that exists in many settings" (347). Their second lesson (347) states:

> A responsive organization will tend, over time, toward an interactive approach toward the stakeholders in its [enacted] environment. That is, dialogue becomes the key to an interactive approach.

To move beyond the traditional view of activists as the enemy or as targets of persuasion means to move from reactive communication to a point beyond proactivity where true interactivity can take place. As activist groups gain size and popular support around specific concerns, the need for interdependence between activists and the organization grows—and with it, the need for interactivity and dialogue. Grunig and Hunt (1984, 297) presciently note that interactive communication "is where public issues management works most effectively."

Two recent examples of the parallel development of interdependence and interactivity—one with external activist publics and one with internal activists—illustrate the generative value of dialogue. In several communities across the United States, police departments are doing more than just reacting to citizens' complaints about the threat of crime in their neighborhoods: Increasingly, members of community activist groups are being invited to contribute substantively to solutions to problems of community security. One solution is the "reverse 911" approach to citizen safety, a system by which police departments can notify citizens when a specific danger threatens neighborhoods or residences, enabling citizens to be more watchful and, in turn, to notify police when suspicious persons or events are spotted.

In a second example of interactivity, AT&T responded quickly in 1993 when employees expressed outrage at a racially insensitive advertisement in the now-defunct employee magazine, *Focus*. Especially concerned were African-American employees, who advised AT&T management that the incident was a symptom of a need for diversity awareness throughout the organization. AT&T executives joined forces with activist employees and instituted a companywide review of diversity concerns and a major training program that continues today.

Activists often are identified with the type of problem or issue they advocate. Thus, some writers attempt to identify activist publics by associating them with key issues and drawing conclusions about the nature of activists from how they advocate those key issues (see Anderson 1992; J. Grunig and Hunt 1984, 321–29; Wilcox, Ault and Agee 1995, 356–59). Gay rights activists, for example, are associated with confrontational tactics, consumerists are identified with boycotts, environmentalists with protests and litigation, and racial minorities with demonstrations and seeking government intervention.

To identify activism with distinctive groups, however, and then to characterize those groups on the basis of how they relate to and represent their concerns, is a short-term and self-defeating approach to analyzing communication with activist publics. As social systems change, concerns identified by diverse groups also change. For example, access to employment opportunities for women and minorities has been transformed over the past two decades to a broader range of concerns, including day care and parental time with children, breaking the secondary glass-ceiling effect and valuing diversity. Moreover, the composition of groups who have a common interest in particular concerns will change over the life of those concerns. The antismoking forces once were dominated by religious leaders; now they are led by health advocates and government officials.

Clearly, what's important for understanding activist communication is the nature of the relationship, because concerns and those who advocate them will keep changing and because activism varies multiculturally. The relationship, as I have argued so far, is one in which activists commonly take initiatives to identify concerns, while organizational members respond to those initiatives. Especially effective organizations will seek out potential controversies as part of their community relations activities. Effective activist communication will respond with a receptivity to activist voices—this means being oriented toward interactivity, rather than toward reactivity or proactivity. The differences among the three public relations response modes are summarized in Table 5.1.

The discussion so far might seem to be saying that disaster response, crisis communication and issues management are the same things. In many important ways they are different, and the public relations tradition of treating them as separate subfunctions has some merit. On the other hand, each of these contexts involves activists, and the similarities across situations are more important for effective communication than the differences.

Table 5.1   Public Relations Stances toward Change

	Reactive	Proactive	Interactive
Role of the "Other"	enemy	target	collaborator
Nature of relationship	zero-sum	zero-sum	non–zero-sum
Communication model	publicity; public information	public information; two-way asymmetric	dialogue

Situational Factors: Disasters, Crises and Issues

Activists' concerns vary not just by individuals' positioning in society but also according to the nature of the situation. Activist publics form in response to a variety of circumstances. The nature of those circumstances is related primarily to the type of events and the attendant concerns raised by activist groups. E. W. Brody (1991) identifies three distinctive but related circumstances that involve activism and risk—disasters, crises and issues.

Disasters and Activism

Disasters are the sudden, unforeseen and damaging events that create an urgent need for immediate action. Often disasters are natural catastrophes, like earthquakes or hurricanes. But they also occur as a result of human error in designing or controlling complex systems, such as the space shuttle *Challenger* explosion or the collapse of a stack of logs intended for a celebratory bonfire at Texas A&M University. Brody argues that disaster communication is fundamentally different from crisis communication because crises develop more slowly and result from organizational stakeholders' actions, while disasters are sudden and largely unpreventable. In both cases, however, persons seeking relief from the organization are likely to present themselves as activists, voicing previously unacknowledged concerns to organizational decision makers and insisting on a role in the resolution of those concerns. Thus, in the immediate aftermath of the 1993 Northridge earthquake in Southern California, representatives for large groups of victims whose homes had been destroyed used news media to present their concerns about slow responses from the Federal Emergency Management Administration and California disaster relief units. Within days they were negotiating face to face with officials responsible for expedited resolution to their concerns.

Activists in disaster situations typically are victims or victims' family members. Their concerns typically are to obtain information, immediate material relief or compensation for losses; they are not concerned, as a rule, with policy changes to prevent future occurrences of the disaster. Their communication methods reflect the emergency nature of the situation: demonstrations before the news media, threats of litigation and confrontations with organizational representatives. What makes them culturally diverse is the very fact that they have been recipients of inadequate communicative attention from the organization: In some way they have found themselves marginalized among all the contending concerns of the organization. As such, they have a set of experiences and meanings relative to the disaster that fundamentally differ from those of organizational communicators.

In some cases, the disaster directly involves cultural differences, as occurred when civil unrest followed the first jury verdict in the Rodney King trial in Los Angeles. Ray Corpuz (1992, 16) called those riots "an important awakening, because it focused attention on the issues of social injustice, cultural diversity, and racial tension and the need for greater understanding between all people."

Crises and Activism

Brody is right in pointing out that disaster communication is not the same as crisis communication, despite the popular assumption that most crises are disasters. Crises, Brody argues, are critical turning points in an ongoing relationship: "Crises occur where issues are neglected or otherwise mishandled" (1991, 176). They originate in the relationship with recognized stakeholders, and unlike disasters, they can be anticipated. Often the communication methods used by activists in the crisis situation are powerful and include traditional public relations practices—information campaigns and media events, for example—as well as boycotts and demonstrations.

The aim of activists in crisis situations is to change an organizational practice or policy so that a current state of affairs will be changed in the future. Logging practices in national forests, anti–gay rights initiatives, product treatments and marketing practices in the tobacco industry, local school board control over curriculum content, safety in the community's schools— these are all examples of issues that have become crises in many localities.

Crisis activism can be generated by disasters, too. An ongoing activist group that formed after the Northridge earthquake, Community Assisting Recovery, is made up of insurance policyholders who have experienced poor service from their insurers. Interestingly, this group was assisted in its organization and development of tactics by United Policy Holders, an earlier activist group that had experienced similar problems with the insurance industry following the disastrous 1991 fire in Oakland, California.

Issues and Activism

Issues are the third situational factor in activist communication. An issue is a controversy that has potential to change public policy regarding the organization. Issues become crises if they are not resolved before they force the organization into a critical turning point, often as a result of policy changes by government regulators. Many writers have recognized the developmental pattern in the life cycle of an issue (e.g., Brody 1991, 183; Center and Jackson 1995, 315). Brad E. Hainsworth (1990) describes the evolution process of issues in four stages—(1) origin, (2) mediation and amplification, (3) organization and (4) resolution. Figure 5.1 diagrams these stages and identifies the relationship between issues and crises.

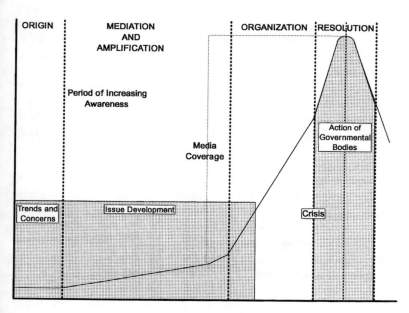

Figure 5.1   Issue cycle. Reprinted, by permission, from Hainsworth 1990, 37.

Issues arise, Hainsworth notes, "when an organization or public attaches significance to a perceived problem that is a consequence of a developing political, economic, or social trend" (1990, 84). Therefore, it is necessary that organizations have mechanisms for including trends in their enacted environments. An issue becomes amplified as groups coalesce around similar perspectives on the topic. Specialized industry media and mass news media begin to pay attention to the matter at this point, and the media attention often further amplifies the issue into a public policy issue. In the organization stage, commitment builds within advocacy groups, the nature of the issue changes from a problem to a policy conflict, and publics become more diverse. Resolution marks the "protracted and potentially costly" (86) process of creating regulation or legislation to resolve the conflict.

The crucial insight from Hainsworth's analysis is that once issues become amplified through mass media coverage and the solidifying of activists' positions, they gain policy implications and enter widespread public controversy. They no longer are issues but become crises.

Issues activism is more subtle, local and manageable than crisis activism. The appearance of an issue is signaled by complaints or demands or letters to the editor by parties usually not formerly recognized as stakeholders in the organization. Customers whose vehicles had been serviced at California Sears Auto Centers in the early 1990s, for example, lodged complaints with Sears and state regulators. Sears failed to recognized those customers as stakeholders and misinterpreted the meaning of their complaints. As a result, Sears shortly had to contend with a consumer relations crisis unprecedented in its history, which ended with the largest customer compensation program ever undertaken by a U.S. retailer.

The engine that produces issues is environmental change. Changes in technology, economic trends, social tastes and evolving relationships among groups can lead to issues affecting any organization. Insofar as issues are socially constructed within an enacted environment, the earlier an organization joins the discussion that leads to the rhetorical construction of an issue, the more influential it will be in the definition and resolution of the controversy.

Moreover, activist communication is not intended to capture all there is of issues management. It has an outreach component, too. Just as diverse stakeholders wish to engage in dialogue with organizational leaders, so organizations must see themselves as stakeholders in the public policy formulation process and strive to become involved in dialogue with policy-makers and ultimately to become part of public decisions. Mary Ann Pires (1988) describes how Texaco sought dialogue with public-interest groups by taking an interactive approach to issues management. Following are the philosophical guidelines Texaco used in this effort (187):

1. Strive for long-term relationships with public interest groups, not expedient encounters.

2. Start by listening to what the groups have to say, to their needs, issue concerns, and so forth. Don't propagandize. Listening provides the clues that can lead to future cooperation.

3. Don't overpromise. [Use] caution . . . , primarily to avoid creating false expectations on either side.

4. Be prepared to give as well as get. To operate any other way borders on manipulation. Reciprocity is a legitimate expectation of all parties to such activities.

5. Treat people decently, respecting confidences.

Treating people decently, Pires says, involves listening carefully to discern others' needs, respecting others' time and schedules, keeping confidences and reciprocating across the board.

This guidance on coalition building from Texaco can help organizations be more responsive in all three situations where activist communication can occur. Those situational factors are summarized in Table 5.2.

Of these three situations, the one in which organizations are least likely to create the desired mutual gain for both stakeholder activists and the organization is the crisis situation. This is so because in crises, positions are polarized, the parties use more radical modes of communication and thus the

Table 5.2   Comparison of Situational Factors: Disasters, Crises and Issues

	Disasters	Crises	Issues
Activists are	victims and families	known stakeholders	unacknowledged publics
Activists' objectives	material relief; news; information	change of policy and practices	discussion/ negotiation
Activists' methods	confrontation; threats; news media	communication campaign; boycotts; litigation; lobbying; legislation	informal complaint; trend behaviors
Source of activism changes	sudden catastrophes	neglected issues; delayed effects of disasters	environmental

stakes are higher for both parties. In addition, crises can be created either by ignored or unresolved issues or by the second-, third- and fourth-order effects of disasters (Brody 1991). This means that organizations should focus on effective disaster response and effective issues management. The best opportunities to engage activist groups may be lost by the time a crisis arrives. But how is effective communication achieved in disasters, crises and issue controversies?

Establishing Dialogue with Multicultural Activists

Several of the principles of effective communication with multicultural activists were set forth in Chapter 4's discussion of community building through dialogue. The responsibility for outreach in community relations coincides with the need to seek out activists who have not yet initiated claims on the organization. Accordingly, organizations should maximize personal interaction, exercise patience in establishing a dialogic relationship and provide mechanisms for activists to voice their concerns.

In addition, the general guidelines for dialogic leadership—recognizing power differences, using persuasion and judgment, being open to others' arguments, holding to a long-range vision of community—apply equally to activist communication. So do the fundamentals of conflict management: being sensitive to the cultural basis of conflict, recognizing mutual responsibility for conflict, accepting the inevitability of conflict and pursuing collaborative conflict approaches.

Many Clear Voices

Many public relations scholars and practitioners have advocated "one clear voice" in crisis communication. By that they usually meant controlling the messages an organization gives publics by funneling all communication through a single speaker. Newsome, Turk and Lattimore, for example, argue that one of the three key elements to promoting successful crisis communication is "the use of a *single spokesperson* during the crisis" (2000, 488; italics in original).

Designating a single spokeswoman or spokesman, however, presents many problems, both practical and theoretical. One person has limited capacity to interact with publics. If the person is addressing one audience, she or he is not available to interact elsewhere. There are also limits to one individual's capacity to obtain and retain information; the "single spokesperson" concept severely impedes the flow of information to publics, violating another maxim, that of the "open communication policy," which is to provide all the relevant information that is known.

A theoretical problem with the "one clear voice" maxim is its denial of cultural diversity among audiences. The other parties in activist communication situations—the victims of disasters, the unacknowledged stakeholders behind campaigns to change organizational practices and policies, and other publics who have issues they wish to negotiate—all potentially differ culturally from organizational decision makers. Their understanding of events, their needs, their bases for trust and credibility constitute a separate worldview and are grounded in their cultural experience and identities.

"One clear voice" also implies that the organization has a fixed version of reality and the spokesman's or spokeswoman's job is to tell or sell it to audiences. In the very first moments of a disaster situation, telling and selling might be the most effective mode of communication; however, the "one clear voice" maxim consistently is advocated as the way to communicate in ongoing crisis situations. Clearly, this one-way approach is not the most effective communication model to use with activist publics, because it limits the varieties of perspectives the organization can take on the problem. Consequently, the range of action options available to the organization is constrained by the model of communication applied with activist publics.

James E. Grunig (1984) has set forth four models of public relations: the Press Agentry/Publicity Model, the Public Information Model, the Two-Way Asymmetric Model, and the Two-Way Symmetric Model. The first two models represent, respectively, propaganda and information giving (both of which constitute telling), and the latter two represent, respectively, consultative communication (selling) and balanced interaction. Despite widespread praise for two-way balanced communication and Grunig and Hunt's claim that up to 15 percent of contemporary organizations practice it (1984, 22), in fact it remains a rarity in public communication. Nonetheless, Larissa Grunig (1992a, 77) has found that, in activist communication, the two-way balanced approach to interaction "offers the most promise for mutually beneficial, harmonious relationships in a fractious (and litigious) society."

Trust and Credibility

Genuine dialogue with multicultural activist publics must be designed to maximize those publics' expressiveness and understanding while maintaining the organization's opportunity for fair and full pursuit of its interests.

Interactivity means not just finding common ground on issues and problems but also establishing common communicative ground, creating trust and credibility through the ways communication is performed. Often finding common ground on issues and problems requires that communicative trust and credibility be established first. Two-way symmetric structures of communication are a necessary start; genuine dialogue also requires an attitude of equal concern for self and other.

A basic consideration in dialogue is communicating so that others will appreciate the legitimacy of what is being said to achieve a common understanding. From the point of view of culturally diverse audiences, this often means hearing organizational representatives who are similar to them in some relevant ways, usually in terms of language and cultural identity. I once met with a group of Hispanic leaders in a southwestern city in an effort to resolve long-standing problems between my federal agency employer and the Spanish-speaking community. My predecessors, who like me were Anglos, had been treated with stony silence and resistance. I asked two of my Hispanic colleagues to go with me to speak with the community leaders. While at first the meetings were not warm and engaging, the parties eventually opened up a trusting dialogue. Together we created novel solutions for the major problems and achieved an ongoing positive relationship. If I had continued with the "one clear voice" philosophy of my predecessors, I could not have opened up a dialogue with this important group of stakeholders. Instead we opted for *one clear but contingent argument* and *many clear voices*, each voice chosen according to the audience's needs.

Trust is created when speakers design communication with recipients' experience in mind, fashioning interaction that affirms audience members' identities, honors their interests, reckons with their cultural orientations and listens actively to their arguments. Arnett (1986) points out that Buber's "narrow ridge" of openness between polarized positions in dialogue requires trust of both oneself and the other. We must trust ourselves to hold firmly to our convictions and be able to change our positions when legitimately persuaded by another's arguments; we must trust others to have a reciprocal concern for both themselves and us and to be able to change their positions in the face of a stronger argument. The key act in establishing trust along the narrow ridge of dialogue is listening to the other's reasons, motives and interests behind their actions and positions.

Credibility, Brody argues, is the organization's "greatest asset in any effort" (1991, 181). He calls it "a commodity gained over time and at great expense in effort and consistency" (182). The following four principles paraphrase Brody's advice about how to establish and maintain credibility in public relations communication with activist audiences:

1. Organizational purposes must correctly match reasonable and rational expectations of stakeholders.

2. The legitimacy of others' arguments must be accepted as relevant to each party's self-interests.

3. Effective communication is required to explain the organization and its mission.

4. Organizational policies, procedures and actions must be perceived by stakeholders as fair and consistent with their needs.

Interactivity achieves these purposes more effectively than does reactivity or proactivity. It is important to recognize three final points about dialogue with activist publics. First, dialogue is not the same as instituting feedback channels. Simply creating a mechanism for dissenting views to be received and recorded does not create interactivity. Dissent must be engaged openly and impartially, with a presumption of trust and credibility.

Second, dialogue does not mean acquiescence to the other's position. Buber was careful to affirm the necessity for commitment to our own interests as a defining characteristic of genuine dialogue: The narrow ridge is a balancing of autonomy and loyalty, of "yes *and* no simultaneously" (Arnett 1986, 43).

Third, dialogue with activist publics is not limited to local or national groups and issues. As world economies become more globally connected and organizations expand geographically, issues, crises and disasters often have international dimensions. Laurie J. Wilson (1990) argues that traditional views of issues management have been too narrow and localized and have been based on cultural assumptions that might not be shared in settings outside the United States. The next two chapters address these problems. Chapter 6 examines how new communication technologies, which alter our sense of place and time, are affecting the possibilities for dialogue; Chapter 7 explores the changing international concerns in multicultural public relations.

New Technologies and Multicultural Public Relations

The computer is an evocative object that causes old boundaries to be renegotiated.

—Sherry Turkle, interviewed in *The Hedgehog Review*

Just after the turn of the millennium, the entire world gave a vast collective sigh of relief—an expression unprecedented in its source and scope—when global disasters failed to occur at midnight December 31, 1999. With a high degree of normalcy, airplanes took off and landed as expected, utilities continued to function, financial markets remained orderly, governments ran as before. The sigh of relief was about the possibility of technological apocalypse rather than an apocalypse of the metaphysical type. The fear that things might go wrong when the calendar rolled all four digits forward was encoded in the unique acronym Y2K—the Year 2000 problem.

Now filled with "Y2K fatigue," we can look back and try to understand some of the implications of the problem and the remedies applied to it. If nothing else, the potential electronic disaster at the end of the 20th century was a harbinger of future problems and a confirmation that the world has become immeasurably more complex as it has become increasingly interconnected through computer-mediated information and communication systems. In this sense, Y2K demonstrates the fragility of our electronically constructed world and our nearly total dependence on it for almost every aspect of public and personal life. At the same time, it demonstrates the effectiveness of the very systems that were the heart of the scare: Fixing the Y2K problem, now seen by some pundits as a global tempest in a teapot, might be the grandest public relations victory of all time, the costliest, most technically effective and successfully peaceful crisis resolution in history. Because companies, governments, industry associations and the media could access unprecedentedly large amounts of information and reach both highly targeted and enormous audiences, they were more effective than ever during the precomputer age in making decisions and providing vital and accurate facts to constituents. Because individuals had access to unprecedented varieties of information sources, rumors did not go unchecked, fears were assuaged and effective preventive actions could be initiated and coordinated (see [*http://www.inc.com/research.html*] and [*http://www.everything2000.com*]). Although some journalists were surprised that all economic systems were functioning normally on January 1, the only adverse consequence of the crisis to individuals was the minor stockpiling of Y2K emergency supplies that some retailers refused to accept as returns.

The Y2K problem is only one of myriad indicators that computer-mediated technologies are changing life on this planet forever. Frances Cairncross calls this transformation "the world's third great transport revolution" (Cairncross 1998, viii). The first transport revolution, dominating the 19th century, was the transformation of the way goods are moved. It took advantage of the machines invented in the early industrial age to move food and products to rapidly expanding populations. The second was the revolution in the way people are transported, reflected in the 20th century's domination by the automobile. At the dawn of the 21st century, she argues, we are well into the revolution that is transforming the way information is transported, and the consequences of this third revolution and the ways in which it will happen are almost anybody's guess.

What is evident, however, is the staggering pace of change in the world's adoption of the new technologies. Less than a quarter century ago, the first practical home computer was placed on the market, when the Apple II appeared. Today close to 50 percent of U.S. homes have a personal computer. According to World Bank figures, the amount of information that cost $100 to process on an IBM mainframe in 1975 cost less than a penny to process on a desktop machine in 1995. Today, five years later, the cost of processing the same amount of information is one-tenth of a cent and can be done in a device the size of a sandwich.[1] In about a decade and a half, cellular mobile telephones have accounted for nearly a quarter of the world's total telephone subscriptions. In the past few years, new electronic devices have appeared that combine cellular telephony and computing, such as palm computers, and innovations that link computers, telephones and televisions into integrated communication systems. In his book *Business @ the Speed of Thought*, Microsoft chairman Bill Gates estimates that the nature of doing business will change more in the next 10 years as a consequence of this third transport revolution than it has in the past half century. Confirming evidence already is appearing, as America Online seeks to merge with Time-

Warner to create the world's largest and most complex communication technology corporation.

This chapter identifies the major technologies that are transforming the practice of public relations and discusses how those technologies are related to the concerns of multicultural populations that might be relevant to public relations practitioners. Primary consideration must be given to understanding the ways in which emerging technological innovations can foster or inhibit dialogue between organizational interests and their stakeholder publics. To that end, I provide a scheme for applying the social-interpretive perspective on multicultural public relations to new communication technologies and expand on prescriptions for dialogue in cyberspace recently advanced by communication scholars.

The Varieties of Technologies

Not all electronic innovations of the late 20th century have directly transformed the practice of public relations, nor are all technologies intruding with equal transformative power, dynamism or potential consequences. Some have had significant impacts in recent decades but have been integrated into the routine activities of the profession and have become stabilized as tools of the occupation.[2] Satellite technology, with its applications in satellite media tours and direct broadcast transmission of images, has changed the way communication occurs by redefining interactional space and the time sequencing of participation. Nonetheless, many of the ethical and practical problems associated with adopting satellite technology already have been settled. Video, including digital video imaging, has become a vital resource in publicity, public information and image enhancement efforts through application as video news releases, video press kits and CD-ROM releases. Cellular technology for mobile telephones and positioning devices undoubtedly contributes to productivity gains for public relations practitioners by facilitating interpersonal contacts and personal transportation.

While these and other innovations (like fiber optics and the proliferation of television channels) have extended the effectiveness of traditional public relations techniques, only the technologies that directly involve the Internet and computer-based information and communication systems are expected to have the most profound impacts on the transformation of public relations and, indeed, on the global society. In this connection, Cairncross (1998, 87) calls the growth of the Internet "the most astonishing technological phenomenon of the late twentieth century." Similarly, in his study of revolutions in communication from ancient to contemporary times, James J. O'Donnell (1998, 9) notes: "The invention and dissemination of the personal computer and now the explosive growth in links between those computers on the worldwide networks of the [I]nternet create a genuinely new and transformative environment." Accordingly, what follows in this chapter focuses on the computer-based technologies of online databases and other Internet and intranet services, including electronic mail, list-serves, Usenet and chat groups, World Wide Web pages and Webnews/Webzines.

Online Databases

To some observers, the availability of online databases is a panacea for addressing society's inequities and improving the role of public relations. Steven Thomsen's study of corporate issues managers found that using online databases enabled them to be more proactive and to develop more effective positions on issues than before those information resources were available. Robert Heath, elaborating on Thomsen's findings, argues that as information-rich members, these issues managers are more likely to be included in their companies' strategic planning activities, implicitly enhancing the stature of public relations in the organization (Heath 1998). Cairncross asserts that increased availability of information through computerized systems will result in better-informed individuals, stronger communities and increased personal freedom. "It will both reinforce democracy and transform it," she says (1998, 257).

Online databases are used by public relations practitioners for more than just acquiring information for issues management. Research on the demographics, psychographics and current interests and opinions of stakeholding publics can be enriched by online searches. Finding information for feature articles, sourcing stories and learning about new approaches to media and message planning can be achieved at numerous expert sites and interactive multimedia CD-ROMs. Some expert sites provide contacts who can be sources of information about special interest areas, such as medicine, business, science, or lifestyle issues (e.g., [*http://www.businesswire.com/expertsource*] and [*http://www.newswise.com*]). In turn, public relations organizations are beginning to establish their own expert sites to make their clients available to journalists and other nonspecialists in search of expert information. An example of the latter is PR Newswire's ProfNet ([*http://www. profnet.com*]).

The use of online databases has not been without problems, however.

Because of the glut of sites and information on the Internet, advanced skill with search engines is needed to navigate the crowded electronic lanes. Standards for truthfulness, accuracy and completeness still are almost entirely absent on the Internet; consequently, the caveat emptor caution is especially relevant to online searchers. In the unregulated environment of cyberspace, the true identity of any site creator or sponsor can easily be masked, making any transaction an act of unprecedented trust. Unequal access to the technology means that as some persons become more informationally rich, others become comparatively more impoverished. These and other problems run like fault lines through all of the public relations applications of Internet and Web-based capabilities discussed here.

Electronic Mail

Globally, more than a trillion e-mail messages are sent every day. The non-synchronized, instantaneous, flexible format character of e-mail has made it the communication medium of choice in the electronic age. Its convenience has been enhanced by wireless devices that permit people to receive messages in virtually any setting. E-mail is now used routinely for communicating on a timely basis with editors, stakeholder publics, legislators, regulators and clients; transmitting newsletters to subscribers; conducting survey research; and managing business functions within an organization.

For better or worse, e-mail also is used for personal communication, and this usage has become the source of the biggest policy controversy for the technology. Employers have cracked down on workers' personal use of the Internet on employer-owned computers during work hours, alleging that personal messaging is an abuse of official property and a misuse of employees' time. Workers in turn claim that personal messages are inevitable, as home life and work life converge in the transforming workplace, and their employers have no right to intercept or audit personal messages. To date, no consistent national policy or state law has been established to resolve this concern, although nearly all the court cases tried so far have gone in favor of the employers' position (Guernsey 1999a).

The World Wide Web

A similar controversy currently brews over whether employees can be restricted from surfing the Web at work. Some firms, like Xerox Corporation, audit employees' use of the Web by monitoring software that records every Web site each employee has visited. Other employers have installed blocking software that limits workers' access to restricted Web sites. While employers have been backed up by court decisions, in a few cases employers appear to have gone too far in restricting employee use of the Web. Lisa Guernsey cites the example of a San Diego police officer who was fired after his employer found that he had visited a well-known pornographic Web site (Guernsey 1999b). The officer claimed that he had intended to visit www.whitehouse.gov—the address of the official White House site—but that he had mistakenly typed in www.whitehouse.com, which brought up the porn site. The city and the former police officer settled for $100,000, but cases like this one point out the tension between worker rights to privacy and access to information versus employers' rights to monitor work and limit use of employer property.

Although public relations has been slow to adapt to the digital revolution, the Web in recent years has been used in countless imaginative applications. Electronic newspapers (Webnews) and magazines (Webzines) are proliferating with dazzling speed, providing public relations writers with new outlets and audiences. Organizational home pages are used for informing consumers and media, enhancing the organization's image, responding to activist publics' challenges and even conducting interactive press conferences. Chat rooms, list-serves, Usenets and news groups are used to mobilize grassroots stakeholders or to respond to critics. And routine public relations tasks, such as sending the local newspaper editor a press release, are easily done online. IBM requires that all press releases simultaneously be sent via the Internet, and the electronic press releases must have hot links to sites that will be informative for their recipients.

Issues for Multicultural Public Relations

While each of the technologies I have discussed presents public relations with undeniable current and potential benefits of a practical nature, each also has unresolved philosophical, ethical or theoretical problems associated with it, and these problems can constitute obstacles for effective multicultural public relations practice. I have organized my analysis into three linked concerns about the effects of technology: the depersonalization of communication, the influence on cultural identities and the construction of communities.

Media and Depersonalization

In her qualitative study of practitioner perspectives on technology, Melissa Johnson (1997, 223) noted that "one consistent theme was how audience-centered the practitioners were in their employment of new technologies." The dominant reason public relations professionals expressed for choosing to use new technologies was to reach new audiences, and they expressed concern for the "comfort level" of their audiences. Indeed, e-mail, chat groups, organizations' Web sites and other Internet media can more conveniently reach specific audiences, such as less mobile or rural populations, than traditional media do, and they can provide new opportunities for two-way interaction. So-called "relationship marketing," where customers interact with companies in a two-way give-and-take instead of simply receiving one-way information, is fostered by interactive technologies (Kaye and Medoff 1999, 194).

Similarly, individuals and grassroots groups can more readily mobilize to influence organizations. Claire Hoertz Badaracco concludes that "technology has . . . increased exponentially the velocity with which an individual can affiliate, organize special interest groups, and create advocacy campaigns targeting elites or officials" (1998, 267). The case of the "Flaming Fords" Web site attests to this democratizing power of new technologies. Many observers attribute the success of a single Web site ([*http://www.flamingford.com/coverage.html*], now defunct), created by disgruntled Ford Ranger owners Debra and Edward Goldgehn, for the then-largest recall of vehicles by an auto manufacturer: Ford Motor Company in 1996 recalled over 8.7 million vehicles at a cost of nearly $300 million because of faulty ignition switches that spontaneously caught fire (see Coombs 1998).

In these ways, the new technologies enhance the reach and influence of all participants in public relations communication and foster democratization. On the other hand, some critics fear that reliance on media to achieve productivity gains and create ever larger and more highly segmented audiences might produce a media dependence that will decrease face-to-face interaction and reduce the use of more personalized technologies like the telephone. Some of Johnson's interviewees expressed a fear that their clients might perceive them to be less personal because they were using new technologies for communication. There is a good basis for this fear. Relationship building is the main objective of nearly all public relations communication: Marlow and Sileo (1996, 168) conclude their tour through the new technologies by pointing out that "public relations is and always will be a relationship business." Building relationships in real time, face-to-face communication maximizes social presence and demands the highest level of accountability from the participants. Social presence—physical closeness and the availability of all personal message channels—is essential to creating open and trusting relationships, and social presence is dramatically reduced in electronically mediated interaction.

It is still unclear what kind of relationships *can* be constructed and what their qualities will be when communication is routinely conducted in cyberspace. At a minimum, those relationships will be built on less-than-optimal intimacy and less-than-complete reciprocal knowledge of the parties. The opportunities for accurate, individualized feedback in interaction are inhibited by the inherent design characteristics of technology: Web sites vary in their user-friendliness, frequency of monitoring, responsiveness of monitors, channel capacity of the medium and so forth. Even real-time multimedia teleconferencing restricts nonverbal channel cues and distorts the context of interaction for participants. In addition, as Johnson's research points out, even among public relations professionals, there are differences in individuals' comfort levels and familiarity with technologies, which often inhibits participation (Johnson 1997, 225–26). Consider how much more profound these differences might be across the various members in the diverse publics who are stakeholders in a typical organization. Finally, there are issues of distribution of technology systems, both hardware and software. Although more than half of U.S. homes now have personal computers, not all are Internet connected, and not all have adequate or compatible Web access software. More to the point, nearly half the households are not equipped to interact by computer, and those have-nots tend to be the less advantaged economically and the less-educated members of society. *Business Week Online* reports that as of 1997, 42 percent of households with computers have incomes over $50,000 a year, while those households with $25,000 or less account for only 18 percent of Web and Internet users. Kaye and Medoff argue that this disparity is vastly amplified in less-developed countries, where "these people are going to be left out of cyberspace for the foreseeable future" (1999, 308). These inhibiting features of the new media that interpose themselves between persons who desire to construct effective, egalitarian relationships must be addressed if technology is to become a truly democratizing influence on public relations.

Identities in Cyberspace

If it is more difficult to establish authentic, fully textured relationships in cyberspace than the old-fashioned way, it also might be the case that people's and organizations' identities are less stable and secure there, too. Consider, for example, Sherry Turkle's study of multiple user domain (MUD) environments on the Internet, an online application in which players create characters and engage in role-playing as a collaborative sort of electronic performance art (Turkle 1996). Turkle argues that the technology facilitates—even encourages—the construction and reconstruction of identity as a multiplicity instead of as a unity, which sensitizes MUDders to the potential for identity change and to the diverse aspects of personhood. While this might seem necessary in a postmodern world where knowledge itself has become destabilized, it weakens the certainty individuals have about the integrity of their own biographies, the worth of their moral sense and the predictability of their social interactions. Kenneth Gergen, while arguing that a fluid, multiple sense of identity might be an antidote to existential isolation, notes that "these tendencies . . . function so as to undermine the longstanding presumption of a palpable self, of personal consciousness as an agentive source, or of interior character as a touchstone of the moral life" (1999, 32). These tendencies are generated in what Gergen calls contemporary cultural technology.

In a broader sense, identity is concerned with being a member of a particular arrangement of groups, and as those affiliations and self-attributions change over time, the sense of personal identity is modified. Identity is functional for an individual only as long as it is comprehensible and cohesive within an autobiography—a story about oneself—that stretches across time; the self as a moral agent and interpretable person is diminished to the extent that one's identity is fragmented, disassembled or self-contradictory. Thus, identity should be experienced as an evolving unity that travels across space and time. As I argued in Chapter 2, identities are constructed, displayed and reconstructed in communication. If, however, the nature of communicative interaction challenges the continuity of one's self in time or space, greatly expands the range of possible realities, increases the array of activities and relationships in which to engage and induces a material, intellectual and spiritual transience, then the unitary sense of self can indeed become disassembled. Gergen comments that "in the new techno-based ethos there is little need for the inner-directed, one-style-for-all individual. Such a person is narrow, parochial, inflexible. In the fast pace of the technological society, concern with the inner life is a luxury—if not a waste of time. . . . [T]he interior self recedes in significance" (1999, 29–30). Thus, to engage in communication that contributes to a fragmentation of, or contradiction to, a participant's sense of self-identity is to diminish that party's significance by reducing that person's capacity for action and moral judgment.

Cybercommunities

"When we forget that community requires working out the demands that 'the other' places on us and the demands we place on 'the other' an innocent form of treachery is invited" (Arnett 1997, 29). What Ronald Arnett means to emphasize in this statement is that community (in Buber's sense of dialogic community that I presented in Chapter 4) is not easily nor quickly attained, because it cannot be community on just our own terms. Community building is the aggregation of relationships, and both the construction of relationships and the process of aggregation require careful interpersonal work to integrate "us" and "them," to bring together what was perceived as insiders and outsiders, right-thinkers and wrong-thinkers. Arnett gives recognition to the essentially multicultural nature of communities and the difficulty of achieving community in relationships based on diverse demands. He reasons that "addressing the complexity of building community in a way that honors diversity requires a threefold commitment that brings together seeming opposites" (39). Those three elements are a commitment to a unique idea or action that pulls diverse groups together, commitment to openness and including new participants who will contribute to shaping the agenda of the community, and commitment to recognizing the limits and boundaries of the community, since all communities must exclude as well as include.

Computer-based information and communication technologies can both foster and inhibit community building. It is clear that connecting with others is easier than ever before and therefore results in generally greater interconnectivity. E-mail makes it possible to transmit messages to many recipients simultaneously and almost instantaneously; the Web can provide information and personal links across the globe and access through countless topic domains and search engines; Web pages, chat forums, Usenets, listserves and MUD, MOO (multiuser-domain—object oriented) and MUSH (multiuser-domain—shared hallucination) games are popular occasions for gathering with others in cyberspace. People who are climbing in the Himalayas or sailing solo around the world can keep in touch with their family, friends and press by Internet connections.

The increased interconnectivity of technology, however, does not guarantee the establishment of community. The essential qualities of these Internet applications are speed, the dissolution of distance and place, and low cost. Of these gains, only the last might benefit the development of communities of relationships. Habituation to speedy connections can engender impatience with more personal, intimate forms of communication: We now

routinely refer to postal service delivery as "snail mail." Yet the work of building relationships and aggregating them into communities of diverse demands is delicate, time-intensive work. Our inability to situate and engage
our electronic correspondents in real time or space gives an otherworldly aspect to those relationships. How surprised I was to finally meet an editor I
had corresponded with by e-mail for nearly a year: She was much taller than
I had imagined, and somehow more tangibly consequential than I had felt
her to be. For our stakeholder publics to be real persons to us, we need to
meet them in our full corporeal selves. In the hurly-burly activity of a typical practitioner's workday, it's often a time-saving seduction to use electronic media to connect with stakeholder publics; instead, true dialogue is what
is needed for building communities, validating identities and personalizing
communication.

Promoting Dialogue in the Digital Age

If dialogue is needed for promoting multicultural communities of interest
with stakeholder publics, and if personalization of communication and
preservation of identities are grounded in dialogue, how can dialogue be
achieved in this new era? One set of solutions is offered by communication
scholars Michael Kent and Maureen Taylor (1998). Kent and Taylor characterize dialogue as a "negotiated exchange of ideas and opinions" that is
grounded in a cooperative communication relationship (324–25). Two
principles guide their concept of dialogue: First, the parties do not have to
agree, but they must share an attitude of commitment to reaching mutually acceptable and satisfying positions. Second, dialogue is fundamentally
about understanding one another, about intersubjectivity instead of objectivity or truth. As such, dialogue is about the process of interaction and the
mutual attitudes of the parties in relationship. Their approach to establishing dialogue in cyberspace expressly recognizes that such activities as "feedback," "monitoring communications" and "responding" do not constitute
dialogue. On these points their sense of dialogue is consistent with the sense
I put forth in Chapter 4.

Kent and Taylor offer five principles for promoting dialogic relationships in the Web, beginning with the need for a "dialogic loop" to open up
communication between organizations and their publics. A "dialogic loop"
is a mechanism on a Web site for publics to interrogate organizations and
provide information and for organizations to do the same for publics. Loops
become dialogic only if organizational representatives are skilled in address-

ing the concerns of diverse publics and are competent, understanding negotiators. In addition, dialogic loops must be nurtured and complete: Participants must be committed to timely, informative, authentic responses. One unaddressed issue for dialogic loops on Web sites is the problem of cultural styles of communication: How are organizational representatives to know the discourse orientations and media uses of their stakeholder publics? Should Web-based communication occur downstream of establishing initial, interpersonal relationships with important publics?

The second principle is that information must be of value to all publics, easily accessible and relevant to stakeholder publics' needs. The goal is to provide information not only to meet the organization's objectives but also to help assure that the publics engaged in the dialogue can participate as an informed partner in creating change. On this point, Web managers must ask themselves if they truly understand the information needs and objectives of dialogue partners.

Third is the principle of generating return value. Kent and Taylor argue that by installing on Web sites interactive forums for discussion, question-and-answer formats, expert resources and similar features, organizations will create an interest in return visits to the place of interaction. By equipping sites with opportunities for publics to access alternative sources of information, such as hot links to other sites, downloadable information and referral services, organizations will be creating a context in which dialogic relationships can be nourished. A truly dialogic Web site will provide mechanisms for others to design the interaction formats and linkages to other repositories of information that might be relevant to concerns the partners in dialogue have.

The fourth principle is to make the site architecturally easy to use and understand. For example, the authors recommend that much of the site's content should be textual rather than graphic, because text loads faster than graphics and often is less annoying than information-poor graphics.

Principle five is called "the Rule of Conservation of Visitors," which is a warning not to provide links to other sites that are nonessential. If Web sites include sponsored advertising that allows visitors to "surf out" or links to entertaining but tangential sites, those visitors might not remain in contact with the site long enough for dialogue to take hold.

While these are admirable techniques for tuning up a Web site, they belie a limited concept of dialogue, even narrowing Kent and Taylor's own initial definitions of the term. I endorse their five principles as sound sense in using the Web; however, these principles as articulated by Kent and Taylor privilege the organization's needs over those of stakeholder publics and will contribute little to the *establishment* of dialogic, community-oriented relationships. My sense of dialogue lies in its capacity for mutual disclosure of identities and positions on the concerns held as important by both partners, validation of the others' identities and needs or goals, and authentic desire for joint action. These qualities are difficult to achieve through communication when using the new technologies. While much work has been done to facilitate decision making in small groups through the application of e-mail, intranets and similar technologies, I have not seen a single Web page that invites publics to join the Web organization in reciprocal full disclosures or mutual personal validation, nor are there anywhere in cyberspace mechanisms for conducting truly shared interaction platform design or problem solving. It is even more unlikely that corporate or government sites will provide mechanisms for joint design and development of the Web environment as a first-order responsibility for creating a site for effective communication to be shared with stakeholder publics. On the contrary, most corporate and governmental Web sites appear dramatically skewed in content and architecture to capture visitors and shape their perceptions, give them information for passive consumption and collect feedback for undisclosed purposes. Clearly, Kent and Taylor's principles would help democratize sites such as these; to foster genuine dialogue, however, it is necessary, as Marlowe and Sileo say, to "press the flesh."

An additional problem for establishing dialogic relationships on the Internet is the relative lack of research and planning that precedes an Internet presence of public relations communication (White and Raman 1999). Preliminary evidence shows that, compared with communication using more traditional media, most PR Web sites are established without the rational planning process that guides more traditional communication efforts. White and Raman (1999, 416) conclude that "in the [practitioners'] haste to take advantage of the Web and to establish an Internet presence, the basic tenets of public relations research, planning, and evaluation are often ignored." In reactive moves to employ new technologies such as those found in White and Raman's study, it is all the more unlikely that techniques for enhancing dialogue will be built into the structure of Web sites.

Summary

Lasting, productive relationships are built on dialogue, and dialogue requires co-presence. Accordingly, my principle for using new technologies in the practice of multicultural public relations is to cultivate relationships by *choosing not* to employ Internet-based media whenever practicalities of communicating will permit. Institutional communicators should take every possible opportunity to engage stakeholder publics in person. Important publics should be met at their locations as often as at the organization's own site (note that a Web page is always and only a location whose rules and structure are under the control of its Web master). Imagine the CEO who has never met her or his employees face to face and has never engaged them in discussion in their work locations, but instead communicates from the first day of their relationship through e-mail, a Web site and other electronic media. How productive, trusting, dialogic would that community of organizational members be? This analogy is parallel to a public relations manager attempting to create an Internet relationship with a stakeholder public. Relationships started in face-to-face conversations can and should be augmented by mediated communication, but dialogue will occur only in settings that permit it to flourish, where identities can be displayed and assessed and the creative work of negotiating solutions to jointly recognized issues can be accomplished.

It should be evident that I consider the new technologies to have mixed value for the practice of multicultural public relations. On the one hand, old ideas of mass audiences and one-way communication practices are being displaced by the possibility of nearly limitless numbers of highly segmented, narrowly targeted publics and two-way communication. On the other hand, it is clear that authentically symmetrical two-way communication does not easily occur in cyberspace, and genuine dialogue, as a foundation of productive communities, is not possible without co-presence.

The technologies that are coming to dominate this "brave new era of public relations" are in danger of dictating what public relations will become (Badaracco 1999). It is a mistake to transform the basic ethos, roles and practices of public relations simply because a technology invites change. White and Raman (1999, 416) note that "although the Web has unprecedented capabilities—asynchroneity, a continuous presence, reach to a mass audience without gatekeeping restraints—and has acquired a mystical and ethereal [character], it is, at a very basic level, another communication medium." Technology is inert, valueless, simply a system of potentialities—until it is taken up by human operators. The new technologies thus are not the danger; we the operators are. I fully concur with Kent and Taylor's assertion that "technology itself can neither create nor destroy relationships; rather, it is how the technology is used that influences organization-public relationships" (1998, 324). Accordingly, traditional concerns for practitioners' values, practices, research, intentions, personal ethics and professional judgment not only still apply in this technologized age but also must continue to govern our decisions.

The new technologies nonetheless have changed the communication environment for public relations, and in no arena is it more evident than in international programs and relationships. By transforming our concepts of time and space, technology has transformed the possibilities of international commerce and communication. The next chapter focuses on international public relations and explores how a social-interpretive approach to cultural diversity can influence the conduct of public relations across borders.

Notes

1. Data on adoption of technologies can be found at the following sites: [*http://www. mids.org*], [*http://www.web21.com*], [*http://www.nytimes.com/tech*], [*http://www.aber. ac.uk/dgc/medmenu.html*] and [*http://www.fcc.gov*].
2. The applications of new technologies in public relations are well described in Eugene Marlow and Janice Sileo's *Electronic Public Relations* (1996). That volume contains an extensive list of media publications and media-related professional organizations. A helpful introduction to Internet-based technology for public relations is found in Bobbit 1995; detailed material on Internet technologies can be found in Kaye and Medoff 1999.

CHAPTER 7

Cultural Diversity in International Public Relations

Country is less salient these days than culture.
—Clifford G. Christians, "Social Ethics and Mass Media Practice,"
in *Communication Ethics in an Age of Diversity*

The need for public relations communication often extends beyond the reach of local, regional or national settings. Union Carbide's decadelong reputational struggle following the tragic explosion of its chemical plant in Bhopal, India, demonstrated that crises indeed can involve international publics (Sen and Egelhoff 1991). Other examples of crises that cross national borders are easy to find, from Dow Chemical and ITT in Chile and Nestlé in Africa to the Bank of Credit and Commerce International and Intel's Pentium III chip worldwide.

Disaster and crisis communication are not the only public relations functions that spill across national borders, though. Today, public relations agencies that practice abroad and multinational corporations with public relations staffs carry out a wide range of communication relationships in a diverse array of cultural settings.

International public relations is a comparatively recent phenomenon. Until about 1970, public relations was practiced almost exclusively within Western Europe and North America (Leaf 1991). The ensuing quarter century has seen phenomenal growth of the practice throughout the rest of the world (Culbertson and Chen 1996). Much of the proliferation of public relations has been due to changes of national boundaries, alliances and forms of government, and much of it has been due to technological changes that have facilitated travel, commerce and communication across the globe (Sharpe 1992). While some observers doubt there is an emerging global marketplace (As the world Balkanizes 1991), communication scholars widely agree that the globalization of public relations professional practice is inevitable. Larissa A. Grunig (1992b, 128) notes that "international public relations may be . . . a necessary part of doing business for the public relations firm of the next century."

This chapter does not provide detailed lists of cultural traits, itemized guidance about etiquette and social expectations or standard business phrases in the languages of other nations. Information of that sort is relevant and important basic knowledge every public relations sojourner to another nation should have, but I have not included such information in this book, for two reasons. First, the quantity of cultural information a sojourner or policy-maker would need is so extensive it would require an entire book for each national culture. Many useful guidebooks and chapters on international management, business communication and public relations containing this sort of information already are available.[1]

Second, the *global/local principle* of international public relations is widely understood and followed, and it makes good sense in light of the complex differences among national cultures. By this principle, public relations professionals are encouraged to set overall policy and institutional objectives with a global perspective at headquarters; at the same time, communication campaigns are designed and implemented at the local level by employees or contractors who are in-country nationals and members of the local culture (Epley 1992; Gordon 1991). While the global/local principle is popular both as a theory and a practical prescription, I will discuss later why it should be modified into a *local/global/local model* of international public relations.

Instead of lessons and anecdotes about cultural differences, the rest of this chapter presents three critical issues for international public relations, based on a social-interpretive approach to cultural diversity. First, I discuss two divergent trends in which the homogenizing effects of globalization in business and communication—the trend toward uniformity in consumer behavior and lifestyle—occur alongside the increasing diversity and fragmentation of populations. I suggest ways these two contrasting trends can be understood and bridged in international communication relationships. Second, communication competence and effectiveness in international public relations are explored from a social-interpretive perspective. Third, I present ways to move beyond the traditional advice that focuses on gaining knowledge of others' cultural practices and using the global/local management scheme: I develop three broad principles of communication policy in international public relations by focusing on cultural interpretations and community building.

Two caveats are in order. First, although I argue in this chapter that certain aspects of culture coincide with national boundaries, it is clear that important cultural differences exist within any nation, such as between the Anglophone and Francophone Canadians or between Catholics and Protestants in Northern Ireland. Moreover, national borders are less important than populations' sense of their own spheres of interest and group membership now that global communication systems are connecting related groups across political boundaries. Second, the terms *international* or *transnational* are not precisely the same as *global*. I have chosen *international* as a way of referring to communication activities that are performed in nations and multinational regions other than those of the organization's or agency's headquarters.

Balancing Diversity and Uniformity

International public relations necessarily involves communicators in multicultural settings and issues. This is so because cultural diversity and identity tend strongly to conform to national borders and supranational regional boundaries. The association of nationality and cultural differences can be understood by considering the dimensions of diversity.

Primary and Secondary Dimensions of Diversity

Marilyn Loden and Judy B. Rosener (1991) identify two sets of conditions that contribute to the ways groups of people differ from one another. *Primary dimensions of diversity* are "those immutable human differences that are inborn and/or that exert an important impact on our early socialization and an ongoing impact throughout our lives" (18). The six primary dimensions Loden and Rosener identify are age, ethnicity, gender, physical abilities and qualities, race and sexual or affectional orientation. For many individuals, national origin can be included among the primary dimensions of diversity. These dimensions, experienced as interdependent core influences, condition individuals' self-identity and worldview and exert a lifelong impact on thought, feelings and behavior.

Secondary dimensions of diversity are "mutable differences that we acquire, discard and/or modify throughout our lives" (Loden and Rosener 1991, 19), which enrich the ways we view ourselves and others without strongly influencing our core identities. Secondary dimensions are almost infinite in number, but minimally include education, occupation, income, marital status and military and work experience, as well as other voluntary group affiliations, which will differ from person to person in their specifics. People differ in their ability to modify or discard secondary dimensions of diversity, and those dimensions vary in the degree to which they are susceptible to modification.

National borders define legal and economic entities, but they also can identify a population's sense of origin as a people. Populations within national borders vary in the degree to which they are culturally diverse on some of the primary dimensions: A few nations, like Japan, are highly homogeneous in race and ethnicity, and many, like the United States, are highly differentiated (Cushman and King 1985). In all but the most recently formed nations, however, one element that contributes to a cohesive national culture is *geopolitical identity*. Language policy, national history and ideology, traditional celebrations, use of technologies, religion policy and even topographical features create a sense of personhood and an interpretive logic shared by a nation's population (Victor 1992, 52).

When communicating across national borders, then, public relations communicators almost always face differences involving primary dimensions of diversity, such as ethnicity, race or geopolitical roots. These dimensions constitute core elements of identity and worldview and thus are resistant to cultural change.

Diversity versus Uniformity

The breakup of the former Soviet empire; the fragmentation of Eastern Europe into numerous new nations based on ethnic allegiances; worldwide refugee and economic migrations; and tribal wars in much of Africa and South Asia all indicate that differences among populations are increasing in number and in their impact on international relationships. In addition, as I pointed out in Chapter 1, many populations within nations who are bound by common perspectives on social concerns are declaring cultural status for themselves and are demanding to be understood in their own terms. Thus, diversity seems to be increasing both within nations and across borders.

At the same time, in some ways populations are becoming more alike. David A. Victor (1992, 9) notes that the global marketplace has created a "universalization of consumer buying habits." Citing observations by industrialists and marketing consultants, Victor argues that cross-border similarities often are greater than those among groups within nations. Young people's tastes in music, clothing and food are fast becoming universal; the global spread of consumer products, availability and use of leisure time, and conformity in lifestyle aspirations contribute to the uniformity of cultural identity. These elements of cultural convergence are based on secondary dimensions but pose challenges to primary dimensions of identity.

Victor theorizes that cultural retrenchment—the insistence on cultural differentiation—is a defense against being absorbed into a global consumer identity. In effect, people worldwide are growing more similar as consumers while struggling to retain their core cultural distinctiveness. Cultural diversity, says Victor, reflects communication preferences, while cultural uniformity reflects consumer preferences. "Thus, as the world becomes more globalized in one sense, the people become more parochial in ways most likely to affect marketing and business communication across borders" (1992, 11).

These contrasting trends have complex consequences. For multicultural public relations, one implication is the likelihood that further economic and commercial ties among nations will not necessarily lead to greater convergence on primary dimensions of culture. The need for effective intercultural communication, even under the global/local principle, therefore will continue to be strong.

In addition, economic globalization does not mean that the world is becoming one market with standardized products and communication. Joyce Wouters (1991) points out that while products and leisure activity trends are spreading worldwide, many internationally marketed products are customized for particular cultural settings. "Forces that call for customization over standardization are customer demand in different nations for different product features, consumer resources, and different environmental factors," Wouters concludes (165). Nevertheless, global consumer-products companies maximize standardization because it is thought to be cost-effective. Wouters notes that in customized marketing, "even though the underlying message, and the theme and the purpose are the same, the style of communication is different and is critical to the success of the promotion" (172). In other words, to global marketers, international communication often is a matter of dressing up in local style a set of business ideas, products and objectives created in the culture of the United States. In this way, communicators are adjusting for secondary dimensions of culture while ignoring differences based on primary dimensions.

Certainly it is important to recognize that people with diverse cultural backgrounds respond to consumer messages differently. From the viewpoint of the social-interpretive approach to communication, however, business objectives, marketing schemes and product ideas created in the United States and exported under the camouflage of another culture's language, popular tastes and social norms will not in the long run benefit either the others' culture or the global human ecology. This form of cultural colonization through consumerism, which is grounded in the secondary dimensions of diversity, can lead to more extreme expressions of group distinctiveness based on primary dimensions of diversity. In creating contradictions between secondary dimensions of diversity and primary ones, global marketing also can destabilize social units by fostering identity conflicts within individuals, families and communities.

Bridging Diversity and Uniformity

Extending the principles of effective communication in multicultural public relations to the international setting can moderate the impacts of the diversity and uniformity trends. First, genuine dialogue means finding common ground while engaging in reasoned debate in pursuit of one's own interests. Many elements of international public relations transcend political boundaries or ethnic group identities, such as preserving the environment, maintaining regional peace and stability and enhancing diversity within the human ecology. These transcendent elements can be useful common grounds at the outset of dialogue and throughout a relationship.

Second, affirmation is central to genuine dialogue. When the active affirmation of cultural identities, participants' self-concepts and the parties' relationship is made a focal communication goal, both secondary and primary dimensions of diversity must be addressed. Hence, more than just the style of communication needs to be adjusted to local cultures in international public relations: The organization's long-range motives, strategic objectives and cultural impacts in the others' settings should be subject to dialogue with locals.

Control, Subjugation and Harmony Cultures

Ultimately, the indeterminant and open-ended nature of meanings dictates that public relations communicators be willing to give up the quest to control interaction and commercial relationships with other cultural groups. The North American and Western European *culture of control* reflects the belief that technology is a tool for controlling the environment and that problems are solved, the future controlled and life improved through the application of technology and self-determination. John McPhee (1989) portrayed the control culture as a scientific hubris that seeks to subordinate nature to the human will.

In sharp contrast with control cultures are the subjugation and harmonization cultures (Victor 1992, 69). *Subjugation cultures*, such as those found in Jordan, Tanzania and Guatemala, believe nature is too powerful or sacred for human control, and technology, while seductive, is sacrilegious. *Harmonization cultures*, like those in Japan and India, see humans as natural elements within a larger environmental system. Technology in harmonization cultures is not for controlling nature but for maintaining or restoring balance between people and the rest of nature.

While this scheme of culture-types characterizes culture as fixed and objective, it suggests that attitudes concerning control, causation, privilege and motives often vary by nationality. In this regard, injecting products and imposing technological solutions to problems with a control rationale onto populations with a subjugation ethos amounts to cultural imperialism. Genuine dialogue requires that the control rationale be identified as an aspect of the organization's culture, and communicators must be willing to give up the control culture's sense of superiority based on technology. For example, Comrie and Kupa (1998) describe how various organizations in New Zealand have been learning how to conduct "Maori public relations" and take the Maori perspective in communication campaigns to create more productive engagement. It might be significant to note that efforts toward more culturally sensitive communication with Maori populations occur at a time when Maori are making historic gains in restoring native rights to tribal assets and in legitimating biculturalism (Comrie and Kupa 1998).

If this logic of the social-interpretive view holds, critics might say, then the very idea of what constitutes public relations and competency in its practice is subject to change within different contexts. Indeed, that is a key implication that flows from an examination of international public relations.

Redefining Public Relations and Effectiveness

The indeterminancy of meaning raises the possibility that effectiveness in public relations communication will vary across national settings. Many scholars of international public relations conceive of effectiveness as achieving organizational goals from the headquarters perspective. Joyce Wouters writes that organizations are successful overseas if they make a profit or enhance their image as an international player (1991, 124), and she portrays public relations as broadly supporting those goals by providing an "essential maintenance, coordination, and trouble-shooting role" (3). Just how these functions are to be carried out is not clearly specified, although Wouters provides a wealth of advice about cultural sensitivity. She suggests throughout her book, however, that public relations has a fundamental marketing role within a selling and consultative communication model.

Ray Hiebert (1992) argues that international public relations effectiveness is contingent on the development of an efficient communication system resembling the ideal at home: "Regardless of political system, the more a nation has a variety of communication sources and a variety of target audiences, with developed media and responsive feedback systems, the more effective will be the communication system of that nation." Hiebert's approach moves us closer to the social-interpretive view, which defines effectiveness as the successful negotiation of meanings that result in reinforcement of the parties' self-concepts, enhancement of their relationship, affirmation of cultural identities and accomplishment of strategic goals. His criteria, however, are framed in terms of a predetermined sort of communication system, one with "developed media" and "feedback systems." A social-interpretive approach embraces improvisation, diversity and emergence regarding communication media, but it has a bias toward face-to-face interaction where mutual disclosure and negotiation take place. Moreover, the notion of feedback systems suggests that interaction is a linear, mechanical process of message transmission and response in sequence, rather than an emergent, dialogic process of forming relationships.[2]

Both Wouters and Hiebert, and a majority of all scholarly and practical guides on international public relations, represent what Carl Botan calls the polycentric model for public relations management in multinational corporations. Botan (1992) identifies two dominant models, the *ethnocentric* and the *polycentric* models, which he critiques with his notion of the *public relations matrix*.

The ethnocentric model places an expatriate manager in the host country to direct public relations activities there, while corporate headquarters managers at home make strategic decisions and closely supervise host country programs. This model assumes people everywhere are motivated by the same needs and desires and are persuaded by the same arguments, and it uses in all host country settings public relations practices that managers believe are effective at home.

In the polycentric model, host country practitioners are given autonomy to carry out public relations programs devised and evaluated by headquarters managers. The home organization's goals and programs, however, "are often not brought into question and the underlying assumption—that the host country is merely a site for fulfilling the [organization's] needs—remains intact and problematic" (Botan 1992, 151). Botan's ongoing review of the literature on international public relations has revealed that a number of broad conditions work together in varying combinations to create a contextual matrix that is unique for each nation. To date he has identified four factors in the public relations matrix: (1) the level of national development, including economic, literacy and national unity development; (2) the nature of primary consumers of public relations services; (3) the legal-political context, including issues of freedom of expression, lobbying and press freedoms; and (4) history and origins of the practice. Botan argues that the practice of public relations in any nation depends on its unique mix of these (and probably other) factors, not on home country assumptions about how public relations should be done:

> To avoid the harms of narrow cultural or national assumptions about public relations first requires adopting a definition of the practice not tied to any one set of assumptions, particularly the assumption that public relations is a management function. We need a view that focuses on the process at the center of public relations—using communication to adapt relationships between organizations and their publics. (153)

Effectiveness of public relations in international settings, then, recognizes that the organization's communities extend beyond the home country's national borders. Effectiveness is inherent in a definition that conceives of the practice as communicating to create favorable relationships and communities of interest with relevant publics. The specific frameworks and forms of relationship building in which public relations workers engage will vary from setting to setting, depending on the matrix of cultural, economic, legal and political conditions. However, its focus on creating mutually satisfying and culturally nurturing relationships through genuine dialogue will help practitioners avoid the harms done by ethnocentric and polycentric approaches.

It would be a mistake to leave the impression that public relations practiced outside the United States or developed Western European nations is always a matter of visitor professionals controlling communication within the borders of a host country. In fact, most other developed and developing countries around the globe have flourishing public relations industries of their own.[3] The ways in which public relations is applied elsewhere—the media, techniques, institutional purposes, publics engaged and education and training—can affect how U.S. practitioners interact with them and can influence the further development of an international profession of public relations.

Beyond Cultural Knowledge

Most guides and textbooks on international business and management, including public relations, are created on the assumption that increasing individuals' knowledge about a host nation's culture is the way to achieve organizational success in the host nation (Limaye and Victor 1991; for examples, see Baskin, Aronoff and Lattimore 1997; Condon 1985; Nydell 1987; Wilcox, Ault and Agee 1995; Wouters 1991). Such knowledge about culture, however, consists of generalizations about a group's behavior and mental constructs, which are often stereotyped: for example, in Japan, one refuses a cup of tea three times before accepting it; Arabs are offended by written contracts; banquet tables in China are never numbered; pointing one's foot toward another person is an insult in Thailand (Wouters 1991). In addition, the cultural knowledge approach to improving international communication ignores the obvious fact that most nations do not have a single, homogeneous culture. Films like "Mississippi Masala" and "The Joy Luck Club" illustrate this point dramatically.

Limaye and Victor (1991) argue that, at a minimum, knowledge of other cultures must be augmented by a nonevaluative sensitivity to diversity. They add that communicators must "go beyond tolerance or acceptance of non-Western modes of thinking, values, and communication practices . . . because acceptance may not be enough. . . . It still may remain essentially a Western paradigm with Western standards, just a little more sensitized" (292). The key question, then, is: How does one go beyond knowledge and appreciation? Limaye and Victor recommend that communication effectiveness be based on the dominant values of the local culture, which in turn demands multiple models and techniques for communication framed within individual cultures.

The social-interpretive approach would not develop a fixed set of communication models and techniques in the international context. On the contrary, a social-interpretive analysis often is least satisfying in providing details about how to act in standardized settings (Penman 1992, 236). Three guidelines, however, can be derived from the foregoing discussion to help public relations communicators build positive communities internationally.

First, facts and values are culturally conditioned. What is desirable, beneficial or socially necessary within a control culture might have no basis of relevance to a subjugation culture population. "Development" is a Western concept with positive values in the West. But elsewhere, development often looks like exploitation and cultural imperialism. Many in the non-Western world's populations reject the self-serving hierarchy established by the rhetorical convention that divides the globe into developed, developing and underdeveloped (or Third World) nations. The 1999 World Trade Organization's meeting in Seattle provided dramatic evidence that the world's have-not nations reject this development-grounded concept of the order of nations.

Second, knowing other cultures' rituals, languages, social norms and values is necessary but not sufficient preparation for forming international community relationships. It is necessary also to remain open to the possibility of conducting business within others' worldviews and effectiveness criteria. Furthermore, the nature, means and methods of communication must be emergent, allowing specific communication outcomes to flow organically from interaction based on the few basic principles of genuine dialogue.

Third, practitioners and researchers should be ready to redefine the nature of public relations situationally. We must leave open to interpretation and negotiation what constitutes the forms and goals of practice, depending on the cultural context. Sriramesh's (1992) ethnographic research on public relations in India demonstrates that the types and functions of public relations activities are conditioned by societal culture. More recently, M. Taylor and Kent (1999) have illustrated through their case study of public relations in Malaysia that Western assumptions about key publics do not always apply in other countries. The authors conclude that "just as notions of democracy, capitalism, and freedom vary from country to country, so too should theories of effective public relations" (M. Taylor and Kent 1999, 141).

Taken together, these guidelines suggest that the global/local approach to managing international public relations should be modified to provide for interactivity through genuine dialogue. A first step is for practitioners and host nation officials to jointly create at the beginning of the relationship a public relations matrix for the host society, including its goals, plans and projects. This array of local concerns would be then honored as initial conditions, or givens, for formulating the organization's own goals, plans and programs. This pattern of relationship, a *local/global/local approach*, will structurally mandate space for interactivity through genuine dialogue in international public relations.

Notes

1. Many informative books about specific countries' cultural practices are available, such as those by Condon (1985), De Mente (1990a, 1990b), Ladd (1990), Nydell (1987), and Richmond (1992). Other volumes focus on principles of management in international settings, including public relations (e.g., Currah 1975; Ferraro 1990; Kennedy 1985; Lowe 1986; Roth 1982; Seelye and Seelye-James 1995; Varner and Beamer 1995; Wouters 1991). Useful examples of problems caused by poor communication and cultural ignorance in international business settings can be found in the entertaining books by D. A. Ricks and associates (Ricks 1983; Ricks, Fu and Arpan 1974). In addition, scholarly research and practical information about intercultural communication can be gained from articles in such journals as *Advances in International Comparative Management, International Journal of Business Studies, International Public Relations Review, Management International Review* and *Public Relations Quarterly*.

2. A review of criteria and extensive references to traditional perspectives on evaluating public relations effectiveness can be found in Lindenmann 1997.

3. For a summary of research on the practice of public relations outside the United States, see Culbertson and Chen 1996.

CHAPTER 8

The Future of Multicultural Public Relations

The guidelines and principles presented in previous chapters can be seen as prescriptions for effectiveness in multicultural public relations, based on a social-interpretive theory of communication. Those prescriptions, however, do not tell practitioners and educators how to get from here to there, when "here" represents a profession that demonstrates low recognition of diversity (Banks 1994; Miller 1991), a poor record of educating for diversity (Fitzpatrick and Whillock 1993; Kern-Foxworth and Miller 1992), low employment of racial or ethnic minorities and other members of diverse populations (Kern-Foxworth 1989) and working conditions that continue to foster minorities' perceptions of discrimination (Len-Ríos 1998). All indications point toward increases in diversity, both domestically and in the international areas of public relations practice. Consequently, practitioners and educators must become more sensitive to this immense environmental change by enacting diversity as a concern relevant to their professional lives and by responding to it interactively.

Once again the key question is: Exactly how is that done? This chapter provides some ideas for getting from here to there, when "there" represents a practice of public relations that is culturally sensitive and characterized by communication based on genuine dialogue. This goal for the future of the field can be achieved only if communication focuses on building strong communities within a more humane global society.

Certainly, from a social-interpretive view, it is not possible to control the future; otherwise, the principles of emergence, contextuality and open-endedness of meanings would be invalidated. On the other hand, through enacted environments, human attention and action do have consequences, enabling individuals to influence and partially predict future conditions. The following comments on training and education, professionalism and ethical communication are aimed at helping practitioners, students and educators in public relations more effectively participate in the multicultural future of the field.

Training and Education

Several meta-analyses have concluded that cross-cultural and managerial training can improve practitioners' effectiveness in culturally diverse settings (Black and Mendenhall 1990; Black, Mendenhall and Oddou 1991; Deshpande and Viswesvaran 1992). The quantitative studies examined in these meta-analyses have gauged managers' effectiveness at meeting corporate performance standards, as well as their adjustment to host cultures, their development of appropriate perceptions of diverse populations, their self-development and their ability to form relationships with culturally diverse others.

These types of improvements are necessary for both domestic and international public relations practice: Training for cultural sensitivity, international adjustment, intercultural communication and valuing diversity is essential to creating personal changes in multicultural settings. A diverse and rapidly expanding variety of approaches to these sorts of training is available,[1] and organizations should assess their needs and select a training modality that suits their conditions.

Barbara Walker's approach to the structure of training for valuing differences, while no longer in the vanguard of management training programs (Lynch 1997), has nonetheless proven itself effective (Walker 1991; Walker and Hanson 1992). Small core groups of employees from diverse jobs and levels are organized as grassroots learning cells by a volunteer leader, sometimes facilitated by full-time diversity specialists. Walker's core groups at Digital Equipment Corporation grew organically from early efforts to get people to talk openly about diversity in an environment that was safe from organizational and emotional dangers—the setting resembled a primitive site for Buber's narrow ridge where dialogue could take place. This approach has been adopted with success by other organizations (e.g., R. Johnson and O'Mara 1992).

Similarly, cultural awareness and sensitivity need to be built into university curricula in which future public relations practitioners are educated. Kern-Foxworth and Miller (1992, 21) decry "the absence of information about multi-ethnic public relations practitioners in textbooks" and note the need for more courses in intercultural and cross-cultural communication. Although McDermott (1991) lists 15 universities where graduate and undergraduate courses in international public relations were taught by 1991, over 72 percent of respondents to a nationwide survey of public relations educators said they do not offer a single course in multicultural communications (Kern-Foxworth and Miller 1992). Sadly, not much has changed in the years since those reports: The studies published by the Commission on Public Relations Education, which were based on a national survey and brought together at the 1998 National Communication Association Summer Conference, gave scant notice to cultural diversity in the profession and in PR education.[2] While authors recommended courses in intercultural communication and "cultural studies" (which typically focus on popular culture and media), no recommended core coursework contains content in cultural diversity or multicultural communication. Further, there is no indication that the survey attempted to tap into practitioner or educator perceptions of the relevance of these areas to effective public relations practice.

This book argues that public relations students should be exposed to the concepts, values, assumptions and research methods of all prominent communication theories, including social-interpretivism. Other important components in a curriculum for students headed for careers in public relations are courses in the humanities, social sciences, research methods, cultural studies and communication ethics (Stewart 1993). It is far more important for graduates to be critical thinkers and responsible, literate citizens than to be skilled in any of the task requirements of beginning public relations professionals. Indeed, one national survey found that public relations executive recruiters do not value highly a specialized degree in public relations: 56 percent of the top public relations firms "feel that a PR/communications degree is 'not important' for a candidate" (Hudson 1993).

If this survey reflects prevailing attitudes among public relations employers, the commission members' hand-wringing over making the curriculum more focused on teaching entry-level practitioner competencies might be an unwarranted concern. A focus that is needed, however, is on the large-scale transitions in diversity of populations and institutions' modes of engagement with those populations. Changing public relations education and practice so that it is more responsive to the multicultural world in which it operates inevitably means inviting differences and dissent into the ranks of practitioners and educators. Corporate and agency executives and academic administrators must welcome diversity among their consultants, employees, faculty and students. Instead of seeking similarity and harmony, we need to recruit people and pursue ideas that challenge the status quo. We should seek out not just identifiable minorities but also persons who have demonstrated a sensitivity to cultural diversity and a commitment to helping others become more responsive to it. A number of remarkably successful organizations, like Sun Microsystems and the Body Shop, have found bottom-line advantages to pursuing this philosophy of employment.

Professionalism and Diversity

Kirk Hallahan (1993) argues that public relations is preparadigmatic, in that at least seven basic models for what constitutes public relations currently compete for legitimacy. The paradigm struggle across the field is evidence that public relations is still in search of its professional identity. Yet research by Culbertson and Jeffers (1992) concludes that true professionalism in public relations is distinguished by the analysis of clients' social, political and economic contexts. Social contexts, they argue, are comprised of cultural beliefs, community contacts and individuals' interpretive frames of reference; two of the relevant political contexts they identify are status differentials and positional power.

These elements, while not the whole of Culbertson and Jeffers's model, are foundational to cultural diversity; therefore, in theory at least, true professionalism includes central consideration of cultural diversity. How can leaders of the profession overcome low awareness of diversity or downright resistance to it among practitioners? This question involves huge issues of the profession's political and organizational structure. However, the Public Relations Society of America (PRSA), whose members currently comprise fewer than 10 percent of all practitioners in the United States (Seitel 1998), should promptly move to endorse certified professional education and accreditation of all members, and those education and examining processes should include critical elements of cultural diversity and ethical communication.

The questions of who should be the accrediting body, what sort of accreditation is desirable, and what level of education constitutes adequate professional training are open to debate, and the debate remains nascent. Brad Hainsworth (1993) suggests that the British counterpart of PRSA can provide a model with its academic and work qualification requirements for membership. Hainsworth also argues that PRSA should both oversee accreditation of university degree programs in public relations and administer certification of professionals. Frank Winston Wylie (1994) counters that the federal agencies with responsibility for accreditation in higher education have selected the Accrediting Council on Education in Journalism and Mass Communication to accredit communication degree programs. Moreover,

Wylie argues, if PRSA both accredits degree programs and certifies graduates to practice the profession, the process would be "a self-serving, self-annointing cooperation which lacks any official status" (2).

Wylie's arguments have merit. If public relations is to achieve true professional status, practitioners and educators must go through the difficult and lengthy process of establishing accredited graduate programs that specialize in communication theory, research, ethics and effective practice. Undergraduate education for public relations should be strongly oriented toward the humanities and social sciences. These conditions are generously reflected in the recommendations of the Commission on Public Relations Education and in Dean Kruckeberg's (1998a) views on professionalism in public relations. To advance PR professionalism, a state certification or licensing mechanism should be established, similar to what is now required for the legal profession and the medical professions, including nursing. Oversight of licensing should be governed by national boards of practitioners and educators who themselves have successfully passed examinations and licensing. With a rigorous professional education and licensing procedure in place, PRSA could become the core professional organization representing not 10 percent but closer to 100 percent of practitioners.

I am less sanguine about the view expressed by Kruckeberg (1998b) concerning the professionalization of ethics in public relations. Kruckeberg's thesis is that as public relations moves toward global recognition as a professional practice, it is inevitable that personal ethics of practitioners will be displaced by a more homogeneous professional code. He likens this process to the evolution of professional ethics in journalism and medicine. Moreover, application of a professional ethical code will be conjoint with and eventually integrated into the ethical standards of the dominant coalition of the PR practitioner's organization. In short, to become professionalized as public relations practitioners is necessarily to become at one with the world managerial monoculture and for ethical frameworks to become universalized.

This prospect would be a tragic loss for multiculturalism, for diversity in organizations and for the practice of public relations. The dominant, universalistic ethical codes in medicine have led physicians to maximize utilization of life-prolonging technologies with scant regard for personal and cultural values of human dignity at life's end. Renegade physicians now are employing indigenous culture-based, alternative forms of treatment along with more traditional Western medical practice. The same universalizing codes have encouraged physicians (against their personal standards of probity and professionalism) to make therapeutic decisions based as much on economic considerations as on the humane treatment of patients. Similarly dominant, universalistic codes in journalism appear to value career enhancement through sensationalism and bottom-line thinking that permit stories to be modified or removed from publication or broadcast because of ownership, sponsorship or advertising interests. More important, the very idea of establishing dialogic communities with diverse populations is inimical to the subsuming of diverse ethical systems under an overarching professional code. Finally, if public relations is to retain its important function as the moral conscience of organizations, especially with regard to social responsibility and interaction with diverse publics, it must retain its independent ethical stance toward public communication. Being a "professional" in a professional occupation is more than being recognized as a distinctive, white-collar enterprise; it also means not being co-opted by other interests and having a clear and unique ethical vision of the practice.

Ethical Communication and Diversity

Effective communication is the key component of public relations education, credentialing, practice and scholarship in a multicultural world. From the social-interpretive perspective, effectiveness always has a moral dimension. As Robyn Penman (1992, 238–39) describes the relationship between morality and communication:

> If communicative action has a voluntary base, then we are responsible for our actions. If our social knowledge is constituted in our communicative practices, the knowledge is of our making and, again, we are responsible. If our knowledge is based on values, then we have incorporated, by implication, what we believe is good and desirable. If these are the case, then our communicative practices have at their heart a moral dimension.

Niels Thomassen (1992) points out that responsibility, as an ethical principle, itself needs moral questioning: "Who is one responsible for? in what way and when? what does responsibility really mean? and where does it come from? If one continues to maintain that the individual can only get to know it by immersing himself [or herself] in concrete situations, then this point of view is difficult to distinguish from subjective opinions" (19). The problem for ethical communication is to identify a standard for responsibility in communication, so that it can be applied across countless actual situations.

Inevitably, communication responsibility involves power relationships. Thomassen (1992, 119) observes that "all communication takes place within a complex power structure." Arguing that the central issue for ethical communication is the proper governance of power and conflict, Thomassen says the standard must be based on equality. It is not that all persons are biologically or socially equal, but the standard for responsible treatment is that "all humans must be considered equal in the fundamental sense that they have the right to a life of quality, that their life should succeed" (119). The underlying ethical principle, then, is equality of consideration in the pursuit of fulfillment, such that no party gains at the expense of others.

From this viewpoint, individuals are responsible not just for their own welfare but also for maintaining an attitude that favors equal consideration. All persons, therefore, whether acting as individuals or as representatives of institutions, must also side with the oppressed, the disenfranchised, the marginal and the humiliated. This is what Thomassen means by *solidarity*—the norm and fundamental moral virtue in communication "is to act in such a way that one shows solidarity for all parties involved" (1992, 120). Thus, the standard of solidarity through equal consideration is recognizable only as communicative behavior, not as a psychological form or state. As an enacted ethical principle, solidarity can be motivated by myriad reasons—love, empathy, rational gain, even fear or distrust—but, Thomassen says, "the crucial thing is that the meaning of an action is determined by an equal weighting of the interests of those involved, or their right to succeed in life" (144).

What solidarity means in terms of multicultural public relations is that ethical communicators must learn the interests of those involved, be sensitive to their equal right to succeed and construct communication as genuine dialogue. But genuine dialogue is possible only when parties approach one another with what Ellen J. Langer (1989) calls *mindfulness*. Mindfulness is more than concentration. In Buddhist meditation practice, concentration is "defined as that faculty of the mind which focuses single-mindedly on one object without interruption" (Gunaratana 1993, 162). Mindfulness "is a pure noticing factor" (Gunaratana 1993, 164), an openness to understanding whatever concentration focuses on.

Langer sees mindfulness as the opposite of *mindlessness*, our all-too-normal state of awareness in which we rigidly adhere to preset categories of knowledge, exhibit automatic behavior and act from a single, narrow perspective on the world. On the contrary, mindfulness is characterized by three key qualities: creation of new categories of understanding, openness to new information and awareness of multiple perspectives.

The quality of creating new categories is crucial. Distinctions of experience that humans learn in the socialization process—such as male/female, young/old, them/us—often become rigid categories that take on a life of their own; when we sort new experiences into existing, old categories, we become trapped in a fixed reality with little possibility for change. Langer's research shows that most young children and highly creative adults continually categorize and recategorize experiences in new ways, as "an adaptive and inevitable part of surviving in the world" (1989, 63).

Mindfulness is that state of mental openness where new cognitive categories are welcome and where readiness to accept new information and perspectives motivates communication. Two requirements seem necessary for mindfulness to be institutionalized in any organization's public relations efforts. First, it must be learned and practiced as a way of being. Trained facilitators should help members learn to become more mindful before more specific communication training takes place. Second, the ethical principles in which mindfulness is grounded should be incorporated into organizational policies and corporate philosophy statements.

In the final analysis, though, genuine dialogue with relevant publics will occur only when organizational leaders personally demonstrate that they ground their own communication in solidarity and mindfulness. Without total commitment to these principles, both across the public relations profession and throughout an organization's membership, true diversity will be impossible. The physicist Freeman Dyson (1988, 6) succinctly described the risk in falling short of this goal: "Without diversity, there can be no freedom."

Notes

1. Publications such as *HRMagazine, Training* and *Training and Development* have featured numerous articles on diversity training, especially since the mid-1990s. The *International Journal of Intercultural Relations* contains a "Training Section," showcasing research articles about intercultural and cross-cultural training. Also of use is the *Diversity Training Bulletin*. Books by Susan E. Jackson and associates (1993), L. I. Kessler (1990) and Sondra Thiederman (1991) offer detailed guidance for designing and implementing diversity training programs. Thiederman's book also provides exercises, tips and a bibliography on cross-cultural training. Planning techniques and integrating diversity training with total organizational change are featured in Leach and George 1995. Roosevelt Thomas's revised view of diversity training can be found in his 1996 volume, *Redefining Diversity* (Thomas 1996).
2. Papers generated by the commission have been published in Turk and Botan 1999.

References

Ainlay, S. C., G. Becker, and L. M. Coleman, eds. 1986. *The Dilemma of Difference: A Multidisciplinary View of Stigma*. New York: Plenum Press.

Alberts, R. D. 1992. Polycultural perspectives on organizational communication. *Management Communication Quarterly* 6:74–84.

Anderson, D. S. 1992. Identifying and responding to activist publics: A case study. *Journal of Public Relations Research* 4:151–65.

Arnett, R. C. 1986. *Communication and Community: Implications of Martin Buber's Dialogue*. Carbondale: Southern Illinois University Press.

Arnett, R. C. 1997. Communication and community in an age of diversity. In *Communication Ethics in an Age of Diversity*, edited by J. M. Macau and R. C. Arnett. Urbana: University of Illinois Press.

As the world Balkanizes, opportunity seems global. 1991. *Public Relations Reporter*, 16 September, 1.

Asante, M., and W. B. Gudykunst. 1989. Preface to *Handbook of International and Intercultural Communication,* edited by M. K. Asante and W. B. Gudykunst. Newbury Park, CA: Sage.

Asante, M., and D. Ravitch. 1991. Multiculturalism: An exchange. *American Scholar* 60:267–77.

Augsburger, D. W. 1992. *Conflict Mediation across Cultures: Pathways and Patterns*. Louisville, KY: Westminster/John Knox Press.

Badaracco, C. H. 1998. The transparent corporation and organized community. *Public Relations Review* 24:265–72.

Bakhtin, M. 1984. *Problems of Dostoevsky's Poetics*. Edited and translated by C. Emerson. Minneapolis: University of Minnesota Press.

Banks, S. P. 1988. Achieving "unmarkedness" in organisational discourse: A praxis perspective on ethnolinguistic identity. *Journal of Language and Social Psychology* 6:171–89.

Banks, S. P. 1994. Multicultural public relations: Organizational and agency perspectives. University of Idaho School of Communication. Typescript.

Banks, S. P., and A. Banks. 1992. Translation as problematic discourse in organizations. *Journal of Applied Communication Research* 19:223–41.

Barker, R. 1993. *Saving All the Parts: Reconciling Economics and the Endangered Species Act*. Washington, DC: Island Press.

Baskin, O., C. Aronoff, and D. Lattimore. 1997. *Public Relations: The Profession and the Practice*. 4th ed. Madison, WI: Wm. C. Brown.

Baytos, L. 1992. Launching successful diversity initiatives. *HR Magazine* 37 (March): 91.

Becker, G., and R. Arnold. 1986. Stigma as a social and cultural construct. In *The Dilemma of Difference: A Multidisciplinary View of Stigma,* edited by S. C. Ainlay, G. Becker, and L. M. Coleman. New York: Plenum Press.

Becker, H. S. 1963. *Outsiders: Studies in the Sociology of Deviance.* New York: Free Press.

Becker, T. E., and R. S. Billings. 1993. Profiles of commitment: An empirical test. *Journal of Organizational Behavior* 14:177–90.

Berry, W. 1977. *The Clearing.* New York: Harcourt Brace Jovanovich.

Berscheid, E., and E. H. Walster. 1978. *Interpersonal Attraction.* 2d ed. Reading, MA: Addison-Wesley.

Biagi, S., and M. Kern-Foxworth. 1997. *Facing Difference: Race, Gender, and Mass Media.* Thousand Oaks, CA: Pine Forge Press.

Black, J. S., and M. Mendenhall. 1990. Cross-cultural training effectiveness: A review and a theoretical framework for future research. *Academy of Management Review* 15:113–36.

Black, J. S., M. Mendenhall, and G. Oddou. 1991. Towards a comprehensive model of international adjustment: An integration of multiple theoretical perspectives. *Academy of Management Review* 16:291–317.

Bloom, A. 1987. *The Closing of the American Mind: How Higher Education Has Failed Democracy and Impoverished the Souls of Today's Students.* New York: Simon and Schuster.

Bobbitt, R. 1995. An Internet primer for public relations. *Public Relations Quarterly* 40:27–32.

Botan, C. 1992. International public relations: Critique and reformulation. *Public Relations Review* 18:103–7.

Botan, C., ed. 1993. Public relations paradigm. *Public Relations Review* 19(2) [special issue].

Botan, C., and V. Hazleton Jr., eds. 1989. *Public Relations Theory.* Hillsdale, NJ: Lawrence Erlbaum.

Bovee, T. 1993. Times are slow for blue collars. *Lewiston Morning Tribune,* 29 January, A1.

Boyett, J. H., and H. P. Conn. 1991. *Workplace 2000: The Revolution Reshaping American Business.* New York: Dutton.

Brody, E. W. 1991. *Managing Communication Processes: From Planning to Crisis Response.* New York: Praeger.

Broom, G. M., S. Casey, and J. Ritchey. 1997. Toward a concept and theory of organization-public relationships. *Journal of Public Relations Research* 9 (2): 83–98.

Buber, M. 1965. *Between Man and Man.* Translated by R. G. Smith. New York: Macmillan.

Buber, M. 1970. *I and Thou.* Translated by W. Kaufmann. New York: Charles Scribner's Sons.

Cairncross, F. 1998. *The Death of Distance: How the Communications Revolution Will Change Our Lives.* London: Orion Business Books.

Carbaugh, D., ed. 1990. *Cultural Communication and Intercultural Contact.* Hillsdale, NJ: Lawrence Erlbaum.

Carbaugh, D., and S. O. Hastings. 1992. A role for communication theory in ethnography and cultural analysis. *Communication Theory* 2:156–65.

Carey, J. W. 1989. *Communication as Culture: Essays on Media and Society.* Boston: Unwin Hyman.

Carr-Ruffino, N. 1996. *Managing Diversity: People Skills for a Multicultural Workplace.* Cincinnati, OH: Thomson Executive Press.

Census Bureau. 1992. *Population Projections of the United States by Age, Sex, Race, and Hispanic Origin: 1992 to 2050.* Washington, DC: U.S. Bureau of the Census.

Center, A. H., and P. Jackson. 1995. *Public Relations Practices: Managerial Case Studies and Problems.* 5th ed. Englewood Cliffs, NJ: Prentice-Hall.

Cheney, G. 1983a. On the various and changing meanings of organizational membership: A field study of organizational identification. *Communication Monographs* 50:342–63.

Cheney, G. 1983b. The rhetoric of identification and the study of organizational communication. *Quarterly Journal of Speech* 69:143–58.

Cheney, G. 1991. *Rhetoric in an Organizational Society: Managing Multiple Identities.* Columbia: University of South Carolina Press.

Cheney, G. 1992. The corporate person (re)presents itself. In *Rhetorical and Critical Approaches to Public Relations,* edited by E. L. Toth and R. L. Heath. Hillsdale, NJ: Lawrence Erlbaum.

Cheney, G. 1999. *Values at Work: Employee Participation Meets Market Pressure at Mondragon.* Ithaca, NY: Cornell University Press.

Cheney, G., and G. N. Dionisopoulos. 1989. Public relations? No, relations with publics: A rhetorical-organizational approach to contemporary corporate communications. In *Public Relations Theory,* edited by C. Botan and V. Hazleton Jr. Hillsdale, NJ: Lawrence Erlbaum.

Cheney, G., and S. L. Vibbert. 1987. Corporate discourse: Public relations and issue management. In *Handbook of Organizational Communication: An Interdisciplinary Perspective,* edited by F. M. Jablin, L. L. Putnam, K. H. Roberts, and L. W. Porter. Newbury Park, CA: Sage.

Christians, C. G. 1997. Social ethics and mass media practice. In *Communication Ethics in an Age of Diversity,* edited by J. M. Makau and R. C. Arnett. Urbana: University of Illinois Press.

CIA's gaffe? A male failing. 1999. *New York Times,* 3 November, A10.

Clegg, S. R. 1989. *Frameworks of Power.* London: Sage.

Collier, M. J., and M. Thomas. 1988. Cultural identity: An interpretive perspective. In *Theories in Intercultural Communication,* edited by Y. Y. Kim and W. B. Gudykunst. Newbury Park, CA: Sage.

Common good capitalism. 1994. *PR Reporter,* 18 April, 1.

Comrie, M., and R. Kupa. 1998. Communicating with Maori: Can public relations become bicultural? *Public Relations Quarterly* 43 (4): 42–46.

Condit, C. M., and J. L. Lucaites. 1993. *Crafting Equality: America's Anglo-African Word.* Chicago: University of Chicago Press.

Condon, J. C. 1985. *Good Neighbors: Communicating with the Mexicans.* Yarmouth, ME: Intercultural Press.

Conference Board study: Volunteer programs "powerful." 1993. *Public Relations Reporter,* 10 May, 3.

Coombs, W. T. 1998. The Internet as potential equalizer: New leverage for confronting social irresponsibility. *Public Relations Review* 24:289–303.

Corbett, W. J. 1992. Communicating in the new Europe. *Public Relations Quarterly* 36 (4): 7–13.

Corman, S. R. 1995. That works fine in theory, but . . . In *Foundations of Organizational Communication: A Reader,* 2d ed., edited by S. R. Corman, S. P. Banks, C. R. Bantz, and M. E. Mayer. New York: Longman.

Corpuz, R. 1992. Unifying the community through cultural diversity. *Public Management,* October, 16–20.

Costello, M. 1993. The latest racist outrage in Idaho. *Lewiston Morning Tribune,* 8 May, 10A.

Creedon, P. J. 1993. Acknowledging the infrasystem: A critical feminist analysis of systems theory. *Public Relations Review* 19:157–66.

Culbertson, H. M., and N. Chen. 1996. *International Public Relations: A Comparative Analysis.* Mahwah, NJ: Lawrence Erlbaum.

Culbertson, H. M., and D. W. Jeffers. 1992. Social, political, and economic contexts: Keys in educating the true public relations professionals. *Public Relations Review* 18:53–66.

Currah, P. 1975. *Setting Up a European Public Relations Operation.* London: Business Books Ltd.

Cushman, D. P., and S. S. King. 1985. National and organizational cultures in conflict resolution: Japan, the United States, and Yugoslavia. In *Communication, Culture, and Organizational Processes,* edited by W. B. Gudykunst, L. P. Stewart, and S. Ting-Toomey. Beverly Hills, CA: Sage.

Cutlip, S. M., A. H. Center, and G. M. Broom. 1994. *Effective Public Relations.* 7th ed. Upper Saddle River, NJ: Prentice-Hall.

Cutlip, S. M., A. H. Center, and G. M. Broom. 2000. *Effective Public Relations.* 8th ed. Upper Saddle River, NJ: Prentice-Hall.

Davis, J. E. 1999. An interview with Sherry Turkle. *Hedgehog Review* 1:71–85.

Deetz, S. 1992. *Democracy in an Age of Corporate Colonization: Developments in Communication and the Politics of Everyday Life.* Albany: State University of New York Press.

De Mente, B. 1990a. *Japanese Etiquette and Ethics in Business.* Lincolnwood, IL: NTC Business Books.

De Mente, B. 1990b. *Korean Etiquette and Ethics in Business.* Lincolnwood, IL: NTC Business Books.

Denzin, N. K. 1997. *Interpretive Ethnography: Ethnographic Practices for the 21st Century.* Thousand Oaks, CA: Sage.

Deshpande, S. P., and C. Viswesvaran. 1992. Is cross-cultural training of expatriate managers effective? A meta analysis. *International Journal of Intercultural Relations* 16:295–310.

Dolnick, E. 1993. Deafness as culture. *Atlantic*, September, 37–53.

Dozier, D. M., L. A. Grunig, and J. M. Grunig, eds. 1995. *Manager's Guide to Excellent Public Relations and Communication Management*. Mahwah, NJ: Lawrence Erlbaum.

D'Souza, D. 1995. *The End of Racism: Principles for a Multiracial Society*. New York: Free Press.

Dyson, F. 1988. *Infinite in All Directions*. New York: Harper and Row.

Edmonston, B., and J. S. Passel. 1992. U.S. immigration and ethnicity in the 21st century. *Population Today*, October, 6–7.

Eisenberg, E. M., and H. L. Goodall Jr. 1997. *Organizational Communication: Balancing Creativity and Constraint*. 2d ed. New York: St. Martin's Press.

Ekachai, D. 1992. Managing multicultural work force: How PR practitioners help corporations improve employee relations. Paper read at 78th Annual Convention of the Speech Communication Association, November, Chicago.

Epley, J. S. 1992. Public relations in the global village: An American perspective. *Public Relations Review* 18:109–16.

Etzioni, A. 1993. *The Spirit of Community: Rights, Responsibilities, and the Communitarian Agenda*. New York: Crown Publishers.

Euske, N. A., and K. H. Roberts. 1987. Evolving perspectives in organization theory: Communication implications. In *Handbook of Organizational Communication: An Interdisciplinary Perspective*, edited by F. M. Jablin, L. L. Putnam, K. H. Roberts, and L. W. Porter. Newbury Park, CA: Sage.

Everett, J. L. 1993. The ecological paradigm in public relations theory and practice. *Public Relations Review* 19:177–86.

Exter, T. G. 1992. Work force 2005. *American Demographics*, May, 59.

Fairclough, N. 1989. *Language and Power*. London: Longman.

Fairhurst, G., and T. Chandler. 1989. Social structure in leader-member interaction. *Communication Monographs* 56:215–39.

Fernandez, J. P. 1991. *Managing a Diverse Work Force*. Lexington, MA: Lexington Books.

Ferraro, G. P. 1990. *The Cultural Dimension of International Business*. Englewood Cliffs, NJ: Prentice-Hall.

Fisher, B. A. 1980. *Small Group Decision Making*. 2d ed. New York: McGraw Hill.

Fisher, W. 1987. *Human Communication as Narration: Toward a Philosophy of Reason, Value, and Action*. Columbia: University of South Carolina Press.

Fitzpatrick, K. R. 1992. Globalizing the public relations curriculum: Preparing students for the new world. Paper read at annual convention of International Communication Association, May, Miami, Florida.

Fitzpatrick, K. R., and R. K. Whillock. 1993. Assessing the impact of globalization on U.S. public relations. *Public Relations Review* 19:315–26.

Fowler, R., K. Hodge, G. Kress, and T. Trew. 1979. *Language and Control*. London: Routledge and Kegan Paul.

Freitag, A. R. 1999. Public relations functions and models: U.S. practitioners in international assignments. Paper read at annual conference of Association for Education in Journalism and Mass Communication, 5 August, New Orleans.

Gass, S. M., and E. M. Varonis. 1991. Miscommunication in nonnative speaker discourse. In *"Miscommunication" and Problematic Talk*, edited by N. Coupland, H. Giles, and J. M. Weimann. Newbury Park, CA: Sage.

Gates, B., with C. Hemingway. 1999. *Business @ the Speed of Thought: Using a Digital Nervous System*. New York: Warner Books.

Geber, B. 1990. Managing diversity. *Training* 27 (July): 23–30.

Gee, J. P. 1992. *The Social Mind: Language, Ideology and Social Practice*. New York: Bergin and Garvey.

Geertz, C. 1973. *The Interpretation of Cultures*. New York: Basic Books.

Gergen, K. J. 1996. Technology and the self: From the essential to the sublime. In *Constructing the Self in a Mediated World*, edited by D. Grodin and T. R. Lindlof. Thousand Oaks, CA: Sage.

Gergen, K. J. 1999. The self: Death by technology. *Hedgehog Review* 1:25–33.

Goffman, E. 1963. *Stigma: Notes on the Management of Spoiled Identity*. Englewood Cliffs, NJ: Prentice-Hall.

Goffman, E. 1981. *Forms of Talk*. Philadelphia: University of Pennsylvania Press.

Gordon, J. 1992. Rethinking diversity. *Training* 29 (January): 23.

Gordon, J. A. 1991. Getting a slice of the "Europie." *Public Relations Journal* 47 (December): 13.

Gordon, J. C. 1997. Interpreting definitions of public relations: Self assessment and a symbolic interactionism-based alternative. *Public Relations Review* 23 (1):57–66.

Grant, D. M. 1988. Cross-cultural crossed signals. *Public Relations Journal* 44 (October): 48.

Greenberg, J. 1987. A taxonomy of organizational justice theories. *Academy of Management Review* 12:9–22.

Greenberg, J. 1990. Organizational justice: Yesterday, today, and tomorrow. *Journal of Management* 16:399–432.

Greenberg, J. 1993. The social side of fairness: Interpersonal and informational classes of organizational justice. In *Justice in the Workplace: Approaching Fairness in Human Resource Management*, edited by R. Cropanzano. Hillsdale, NJ: Lawrence Erlbaum.

Grunig, J. E. 1984. Organizations, environments, and models of public relations. *Public Relations Research and Education* 1:6–29.

Grunig, J. E., ed. 1992. *Excellence in Public Relations and Communication Management*. Hillsdale, NJ: Lawrence Erlbaum.

Grunig, J. E., and T. Hunt. 1984. *Managing Public Relations*. New York: Holt, Rinehart and Winston.

Grunig, J. E., and J. White. 1992. The effect of worldviews on public relations theory and practice. In *Excellence in Public Relations and Communication Management*, edited by J. E. Grunig. Hillsdale, NJ: Lawrence Erlbaum.

Grunig, L. A. 1992a. Toward the philosophy of public relations. In *Rhetorical and Critical Approaches to Public Relations*, edited by E. L. Toth and R. L. Heath. Hillsdale, NJ: Lawrence Erlbaum.

Grunig, L. A. 1992b. Strategic public relations constituencies on a global scale. *Public Relations Review* 18:127–36.

Grunig, L. A., J. E. Grunig, and W. P. Ehling. 1992. What is effective organization? In *Excellence in Public Relations and Communication Management,* edited by J. E. Grunig. Hillsdale, NJ: Lawrence Erlbaum.

Gudykunst, W. B. 1987. Cross-cultural comparisons. In *Handbook of Communication Science,* edited by C. Berger and S. Chaffee. Newbury Park, CA: Sage.

Gudykunst, W. B. 1989. Cultural variability in ethnolinguistic identity. In *Language, Communication, and Culture: Current Directions,* edited by S. Ting-Toomey and F. Korzenny. Newbury Park, CA: Sage.

Gudykunst, W. B. 1991. *Bridging Differences: Effective Intergroup Communication.* Newbury Park, CA: Sage.

Gudykunst, W. B. 1993. Toward a theory of effective interpersonal and intergroup communication: An anxiety/uncertainty management (AUM) perspective. In *Intercultural Communication Competence,* edited by R. L. Wiseman and J. Koester. Newbury Park, CA: Sage.

Gudykunst, W. B., and T. Nishida. 1989. Theoretical perspectives for studying intercultural communication. In *Handbook of International and Intercultural Communication,* edited by M. K. Asante and W. B. Gudykunst. Newbury Park, CA: Sage.

Guernsey, L. 1999a. What employers can view at work. *New York Times,* 16 December, D10.

Guernsey, L. 1999b. The web: New ticket to a pink slip. *New York Times,* 16 December, D1, D8.

Gumperz, J., ed. 1982. *Language and Social Identity.* Cambridge: Cambridge University Press.

Gunaratana, H. 1993. *Mindfulness in Plain English.* Boston: Wisdom Publications.

Gutman, A., ed. 1994. *Multiculturalism: Examining the Politics of Recognition.* Princeton, NJ: Princeton University Press.

Hainsworth, B. E. 1990. The distribution of advantages and disadvantages. *Public Relations Review* 16:33–39.

Hainsworth, B. E. 1993. Commentary: Professionalism in public relations. *Public Relations Review* 19:311–14.

Hallahan, K. 1993. The paradigm struggle and public relations practice. *Public Relations Review* 19:197–205.

Harris, P. R., and R. T. Moran. 1996. *Managing Cultural Differences.* 4th ed. Houston, TX: Gulf Publishing Co.

Hatfield, J. D., and R. C. Huseman. 1982. Perceptual congruence about communication as related to satisfaction: Moderating effects of individual characteristics. *Academy of Management Journal* 25:349–58.

Heath, R. L. 1992. Critical perspectives on public relations. In *Rhetorical and Critical Approaches to Public Relations,* edited by E. L. Toth and R. L. Heath. Hillsdale, NJ: Lawrence Erlbaum.

Heath, R. L. 1993. A rhetorical approach to zones of meaning and organizational prerogatives. *Public Relations Review* 19:141–55.

Heath, R. L. 1998. New communication technologies: An issues management point of view. *Public Relations Review* 24:273–88.

Heath, R. L., ed. 1988. *Strategic Issues Management: How Organizations Influence and Respond to Public Interests and Policies.* San Francisco: Jossey-Bass.

Henderson, J. K. 1998. Negative connotations in the use of the term "public relations" in the print media. *Public Relations Review* 24:45–54.

Hiebert, R. E. 1992. Global public relations in a post-communist world: A new model. *Public Relations Review* 18:117–26.

Hirokawa, R., and K. Rost. 1992. Effective group decision making in organizations. *Management Communication Quarterly* 5:267–88.

Hirsch, E. Jr., J. F. Kett, and J. Trefill. 1993. *The Dictionary of Cultural Literacy.* 2d ed. Boston: Houghton Mifflin.

Hocker, J., and W. W. Wilmot. 1995. Interpersonal Conflict. 4th ed. Dubuque, IA: Wm. C. Brown.

Holt, J., and D. M. Keats. 1992. Work cognitions in multicultural interaction. *Journal of Cross-Cultural Psychology* 23 (4): 421–43.

Hudson, R. A. 1980. *Sociolinguistics.* Cambridge: Cambridge University Press.

Hutton, J. G. 1999. The definition, dimensions, and domain of public relations. *Public Relations Review* 25:199–214.

Is PR degree valuable? Recruiters, APR program not supportive. 1993. *Public Relations News,* 8 February, 5.

Jablin, F. M. 1979. Superior-subordinate communication: The state of the art. *Psychological Bulletin* 86:1201–22.

Jablin, F. M. 1985. Organizational entry, assimilation, and exit. In *Handbook of Organizational Communication: An Interdisciplinary Perspective,* edited by F. M. Jablin, L. L. Putnam, K. H. Roberts, and L. W. Porter. Newbury Park, CA: Sage.

Jackson, P. 1993. Can community relations be the *core* of PR programming? *PR Reporter,* 19 July, 1.

James, K. 1993. The social context of organizational justice: Cultural, intergroup, and structural effects on justice behaviors and perceptions. In *Justice in the Workplace: Approaching Fairness in Human Resource Management,* edited by R. Cropanzano. Hillsdale, NJ: Lawrence Erlbaum.

Jamieson, D., and J. O'Mara. 1991. *Managing Workforce 2000: Gaining the Diversity Advantage.* San Francisco: Jossey-Bass.

Jandt, F. 1998. *Intercultural Communication: An Introduction.* 2d ed. Thousand Oaks, CA: Sage.

Jensen, R. 1992. Fighting objectivity: The illusion of journalistic objectivity in coverage of the Persian Gulf War. *Journal of Communication Inquiry* 16:20–32.

Johnson, M. A. 1997. Public relations and technology: Practitioner perspectives. *Journal of Public Relations Research* 9:213–36.

Johnson, R. B., and J. O'Mara. 1992. Shedding new light on diversity training. *Training and Development,* May, 45–52.

Johnston, W. B., and A. H. Packer. 1987. *Workforce 2000: Work and Workers for the Twenty-First Century.* Indianapolis: Hudson Institute.

Katz, I. 1981. *Stigma: A Social Psychological Analysis.* Hillsdale, NJ: Lawrence Erlbaum.

Kaye, B. K., and N. J. Medoff. 1999. *The World Wide Web: A Mass Communication Perspective.* Mountain View, CA: Mayfield Publishing Co.

Kellner, D. 1992. *The Persian Gulf TV War.* Boulder, CO: Westview Press.

Kennedy, G. 1985. *Doing Business Abroad.* New York: Simon and Schuster.

Kent, M. L., and M. Taylor. 1998. Building dialogic relationships through the World Wide Web. *Public Relations Review* 24:321–34.

Kepnes, S. 1992. *The Text as Thou: Martin Buber's Dialogical Hermeneutics and Narrative Theology.* Bloomington: Indiana University Press.

Kern-Foxworth, M. 1989. Status and roles of minority public relations practitioners. *Public Relations Review* 15:36–47.

Kern-Foxworth, M. 1990. Ethnic inclusiveness in public relations textbooks and reference books. *Howard Journal of Communications* 2:226–37.

Kern-Foxworth, M., and D. A. Miller. 1992. Embracing multicultural diversity: A preliminary examination of public relations education. Paper read at annual conference of the International Communication Association, May, Miami, Florida.

Kessler, L. I. 1990. *Managing Diversity in an Equal Opportunity Workplace.* Washington, DC: National Foundation for the Study of Employment Policy.

Kikoski, J. F., and C. K. Kikoski. 1996. *Reflexive Communication in the Culturally Diverse Workplace.* Westport, CT: Quorum Books.

Kim, Y. Y. 1988. On theorizing intercultural communication. In *Theories in Intercultural Communication,* edited by Y. Y. Kim and W. B. Gudykunst. Newbury Park, CA: Sage.

Kim, Y. Y., and W. B. Gudykunst, eds. 1988. *Theories in Intercultural Communication.* Newbury Park, CA: Sage.

Kohn, A. 1986. How to succeed without even vying. *Psychology Today,* September, 22–28.

Kress, G., and B. Hodge. 1979. *Language as Ideology.* London: Routledge and Kegan Paul.

Kristol, I. 1991. The tragedy of multiculturalism. *Wall Street Journal,* 31 July, A12.

Kroeber, A. L., and C. Kluckhohn. 1952. *Culture: A Critical Review of Concepts and Definitions.* Cambridge: Harvard University Press.

Kruckeberg, D. 1998a. The future of public relations education: Some recommendations. *Public Relations Review* 24:235–48.

Kruckeberg, D. 1998b. Future reconciliation of multicultural perspectives in public relations ethics. *Public Relations Quarterly* 23 (1): 45–48.

Kruckeberg, D., and K. Starck. 1988. *Public Relations and Community: A Reconstructed Theory.* New York: Praeger.

Labov, W. 1972. *Sociolinguistic Patterns.* Philadelphia: University of Pennsylvania Press.

Lach, J. 1999. Diversity in a virtual world. *American Demographics,* [*http://www.demographics.com/publications/ad/99_9907_ad990705c.htm*].

Ladd, J. 1990. *Subject: India: A Semester Abroad.* Yarmouth, ME: Intercultural Press.

Langer, E. J. 1989. *Mindfulness.* Reading, MA: Addison-Wesley.

Larkey, L. K. 1993. Research review and critique of trends in managing cultural diversity. Paper read at annual conference of Western States Communication Association, February, Albuquerque.

Lawler, E. E. III. 1993. *Strategic Pay: Aligning Organizational Strategies and Pay Systems.* San Francisco: Jossey-Bass.

Leach, J., and B. George. 1995. *A Practical Guide to Working with Diversity: The Process, the Tools, the Resources.* New York: AMACOM.

Leaf, R. 1991. International public relations. In *Lesly's Handbook of Public Relations and Communications,* 4th ed., edited by P. Lesly. Chicago: Probus Publishing Co.

Leeds-Hurwitz, W. 1992. Forum introduction: Social approaches to interpersonal communication. *Communication Theory* 2:131–39.

Len-Ríos, M. E. 1998. Minority public relations practitioner perceptions. *Public Relations Review* 24:535–55.

Lesly, P. 1992. Coping with opposition groups. *Public Relations Review* 18:325–34.

Limaye, M. R., and D. A. Victor. 1991. Cross-cultural business communication: State of the art and hypotheses for the 1990s. *Journal of Business Communication* 28:277–99.

Lindenmann, W. K. 1997. Setting minimum standards for measuring public relations effectiveness. *Public Relations Review* 23:391–408.

Loden, M., and J. B. Rosener. 1991. *Workforce America! Managing Employee Diversity as a Vital Resource.* Homewood, IL: Business One Irwin.

Lott, J. T. 1993. Do United States racial/ethnic categories still fit? *Population Today* 21 (January): 6–7.

Lowe, V. 1986. *Asian PR.* Singapore: Times Books International.

Lustig, M., and J. Koester. 1999. *Intercultural Competence: Interpersonal Communication across Cultures.* 3d ed. New York: HarperCollins.

Lynch, F. 1997. *The Diversity Machine: The Drive to Change the "White Male Workplace."* New York: Free Press.

Marlow, E., and J. Sileo. 1996. *Electronic Public Relations.* Belmont, CA: Wadsworth Publishing.

Marston, J. E. 1963. *The Nature of Public Relations.* New York: McGraw-Hill.

Martin, J. N., ed. 1989. Intercultural communication competence. *International Journal of Intercultural Relations* 13.

Matveyev, V. 1991. The oddities of public relations in the USSR in the situation of "interim" economy and politics. *International Public Relations Review* 14: 24–26.

McDermott, P. M. 1991. International public relations in the United States: First steps in a global journey. *International Public Relations Review* 14:37–39.

McElreath, M. P. 1993. *Managing Systematic and Ethical Public Relations.* Dubuque, IA: Brown and Benchmark.

McElreath, M. P., and J. M. Blamphin. 1994. Partial answers to priority research questions—and gaps—found in the Public Relations Society of America's body of knowledge. *Journal of Public Relations Research* 6:69–103.

McPhee, J. 1989. *The Control of Nature.* New York: Farrar Straus Giroux.

Mey, J. 1985. *Whose Language? A Study in Linguistic Pragmatics.* Philadelphia: John Benjamins Publishing.

Mickey, T. J. 1995. *Sociodrama: An Interpretive Theory for the Practice of Public Relations.* New York: University Press of America.

Mickey, T. J. 1997. A postmodern view of public relations: Sign and reality. *Public Relations Review* 23:271–84.

Miller, D. 1991. Multicultural diversity: The communications challenge of the 1990s; a PRSA Issue Paper. New York: PRSA Foundation.

Miller, D. 1993. *Multicultural Communications: A Bibliography.* New York: PRSA Foundation.

Morton, L. 1997. Targeting minority publics. *Public Relations Quarterly* 42 (2): 23–28.

Mumby, D. K. 1988. *Communication and Power in Organizations: Discourse, Ideology, and Domination.* Norwood, NJ: Ablex.

Mumby, D. K., ed. 1993. *Narrative and Social Control: Critical Perspectives.* Newbury Park, CA: Sage.

Nadler, L., M. Nadler, and B. Broome. 1985. Culture and the management of conflict situations. In *Communication, Culture, and Organizational Processes,* edited by W. B. Gudykunst, L. Stewart, and S. Ting-Toomey. Beverly Hills, CA: Sage.

Neff, B. D. 1998. Harmonizing global relations: A speech act theory analysis of PRForum. *Public Relations Review* 24:351–76.

Newsome, D., A. Scott, and J. V. Turk. 1993. *This Is PR: The Realities of Public Relations.* 5th ed. Belmont, CA: Wadsworth Publishing.

Newsome, D., J. V. Turk, and D. Kruckeberg. 2000. *This Is PR: The Realities of Public Relations.* 7th ed. Belmont, CA: Wadsworth Publishing.

Nydell, M. K. 1987. *Understanding Arabs: A Guide for Westerners.* Yarmouth, ME: Intercultural Press.

O'Donnell, J. J. 1998. *Avatars of the Word: From Papyrus to Cyberspace.* Cambridge: Harvard University Press.

O'Dwyer, J. 1994. Multicultural communications—wave of the future? *O'Dwyer's PR Services* 8 (January): 6.

Pacanowsky, M. 1988. Communication in the empowering organization. In *Communication Yearbook* no. 11, edited by J. Anderson. Newbury Park, CA: Sage.

Pavlik, J. 1987. *Public Relations: What Research Tells Us.* Newbury Park, CA: Sage.

Penman, R. 1992. Good theory and good practice: An argument in progress. *Communication Theory* 2:234–50.

Pires, M. A. 1988. Building coalitions with external constituencies. In *Strategic Issues Management,* edited by R. L. Heath. San Francisco: Jossey-Bass.

Pollard, K. 1993. Faster growth, more diversity in U.S. projections. *Population Today,* February, 3, 10.

Post, J. E., and P. C. Kelley. 1988. Lessons from the learning curve: The past, present, and future of issues management. In *Strategic Issues Management,* edited by R. L. Heath and Associates. San Francisco: Jossey-Bass.

Putnam, L. 1983. The interpretive perspective: An alternative to functionalism. In *Communication and Organization: An Interpretive Approach,* edited by L. L. Putnam and M. E. Pacanowsky. Beverly Hills, CA: Sage.

Ravitch, D. 1990. Multiculturalism: *e pluribus plures. American Scholar* 59:337–54.

Richmond, Y. 1992. *From Nyet to Da: Understanding the Russians.* Yarmouth, ME: Intercultural Press.

Ricks, D. A. 1983. *Big Business Blunders: Mistakes in Multinational Marketing.* Homewood, IL: Dow-Jones Irwin.

Ricks, D. A., M. Y. C. Fu, and J. S. Arpan. 1974. *International Business Blunders.* 2d ed. Columbus, OH: GRID.

Roth, R. F. 1982. *International Marketing Communications.* Chicago: Crain Books.

Schiffrin, D. 1990. The management of a co-operative self during argument: The role of opinions and stories. In *Conflict Talk: Sociolinguistic Investigations of Arguments and Conversations,* edited by A. Grimshaw. Cambridge: Cambridge University Press.

Schlesinger, A. Jr. 1992. *The Disuniting of America: Reflections on a Multicultural Society.* New York: W. W. Norton.

Schneider, S. 1991. Managing boundaries in organizations. In *Organizations on the Couch: Clinical Perspectives on Organizational Behavior and Change,* edited by M. F. R. Kets de Vries. San Francisco: Jossey-Bass.

Schur, E. 1980. *The Politics of Deviance: Stigma Contests and the Uses of Power.* Englewood Cliffs, NJ: Prentice-Hall.

Scollon, R., and S. W. Scollon. 1995. *Intercultural Communication: A Discourse Approach.* Oxford: Blackwell.

Seelye, N., and A. Seelye-James. 1995. *Culture Clash: Managing in a Multicultural World.* Lincolnwood, IL: NTC Contemporary Publishing.

Seitel, F. 1998. *The Practice of Public Relations.* 7th ed. New York: Macmillan.

Sen, F., and W. G. Egelhoff. 1991. Six years and counting: Learning from crisis management at Bhopal. *Public Relations Review* 17:69–83.

Sennett, R. 1976. *The Fall of Public Man: On the Social Psychology of Capitalism.* New York: Vintage Books.

Sharpe, M. L. 1992. The impact of social and cultural conditioning on global public relations. *Public Relations Review* 18:103–8.

Skriloff, L. 1997. Marketing to minority audiences. *Public Relations Tactics* 4 (3): 30–31.

Smircich, L., and R. J. Chesser. 1981. Superiors' and subordinates' perceptions of performance: Beyond disagreement. *Academy of Management Journal* 24:198–205.

Spicer, C. 1997. *Organizational Public Relations: A Political Perspective.* Mahwah, NJ: Lawrence Erlbaum.

Spitzberg, B. 1983. Communication competence as knowledge, skill, and impression. *Communication Education* 32:323–29.

Spitzberg, B., and W. Cupach. 1984. *Interpersonal Communication Competence.* Beverly Hills, CA: Sage.

Spitzberg, B., and W. Cupach. 1989. *Handbook of Interpersonal Competence Research.* New York: Springer Verlag.

Sriramesh, K. 1992. Societal culture and public relations: Ethnographic evidence from India. *Public Relations Review* 18:201–11.

Steinfels, P. 1993. More diversity than harmony. *New York Times,* 7 September, A13.

Stewart, L. P. 1985. Subjective culture and organizational decision-making. In *Communication, Culture, and Organizational Processes,* edited by W. B. Gudykunst, L. P. Stewart, and S. Ting-Toomey. Beverly Hills, CA: Sage.

Stewart, L. P. 1993. Ethical issues in organizational diversity. Paper read at annual conference of International Communication Association, May, Washington, D.C.

Tajfel, H. 1978. *Differentiation between Social Groups.* London: Academic Press.

Tajfel, H., ed. 1982. *Social Identity and Intergroup Relations.* Cambridge: Cambridge University Press.

Tajfel, H., and J. C. Turner. 1979. An integrative theory of intergroup conflict. In *The Social Psychology of Intergroup Relations,* edited by W. C. Austin and S. Worchel. Monterey, CA: Brooks/Cole.

Taylor, C. 1992. *Multiculturalism and "the Politics of Recognition."* Princeton, NJ: Princeton University Press.

Taylor, M., and M. L. Kent. 1999. Challenging assumptions of international public relations: When government is the most important public. *Public Relations Review* 25:131–44.

Thiederman, S. 1991. *Bridging Cultural Barriers for Corporate Success: How to Manage the Multicultural Work Force.* New York: Lexington Books.

Thomas, R. R. Jr. 1991. *Beyond Race and Gender: Unleashing the Power of Your Total Workforce by Managing Diversity.* New York: AMACOM, American Management Association.

Thomas, R. R. Jr. 1992. Managing diversity: A conceptual framework. In *Diversity in the Workplace: Human Resource Initiatives,* edited by S. E. Jackson. New York: Guilford Press.

Thomas, R. R. Jr. 1996. *Redefining Diversity.* New York: AMACOM, American Management Association.

Thomassen, N. 1992. *Communicative Ethics in Theory and Practice.* New York: St. Martin's Press.

Ting-Toomey, S. 1985. Toward a theory of conflict and culture. In *Communication, Culture, and Organizational Processes,* edited by W. B. Gudykunst, L. P. Stewart, and S. Ting-Toomey. Beverly Hills, CA: Sage.

Ting-Toomey, S. 1993. Communicative resourcefulness: An identity negotiation perspective. In *Intercultural Communication Competence,* edited by R. L. Wiseman and J. Koester. Beverly Hills, CA: Sage.

Ting-Toomey, S. 1994. Managing intercultural conflict competently. In *Intercultural Communication: A Reader,* 7th ed., edited by L. Samovar and R. Porter. Belmont, CA: Wadsworth Publishing.

Tompkins, P. K., and G. Cheney. 1985. Communication and unobtrusive control in contemporary organizations. In *Organizational Communication: Traditional Themes and New Directions,* edited by R. D. McPhee and P. K. Tompkins. Beverly Hills, CA: Sage.

Toth, E. L. 1992. The case for pluralistic studies of public relations: Rhetorical, critical, and systems perspectives. In *Rhetorical and Critical Approaches to Public Relations,* edited by E. L. Toth and R. L. Heath. Hillsdale, NJ: Lawrence Erlbaum.

Toth, E. L., and R. L. Heath, eds. 1992. *Rhetorical and Critical Approaches to Public Relations.* Hillsdale, NJ: Lawrence Erlbaum.

Triandis, H. 1972. *The Analysis of Subjective Culture.* New York: Wiley-Interscience.

Trinh, T. 1991. *When the Moon Waxes Red: Representation, Gender and Cultural Politics.* New York: Routledge.

Trompenaars, F. 1994. *Riding the Waves of Culture: Understanding Diversity in Global Business.* Burr Ridge, IL: Irwin Professional Publications.

Trujillo, N. 1987. Implications of interpretive approaches for organizational communication research and practice. In *Organization ↔ Communication: Emerging Perspectives II,* edited by L. Thayer. Norwood, NJ: Ablex.

Turk, J. V., and C. Botan, eds. 1999. Special issue: Education. *Public Relations Review* 25 (spring).

Turkle, S. 1996. Parallel lives: Working on identity in virtual space. In *Constructing the Self in a Mediated World,* edited by D. Grodin and T. J. Lindlof. Thousand Oaks, CA: Sage.

Van Maanen, J. 1977. Experiencing organization: Notes on the meaning of careers and socialization. In *Organizational Careers: Some New Perspectives.* New York: John Wiley.

Varner, I., and L. Beamer. 1995. *Intercultural Communication in the Global Workplace.* Chicago: Irwin.

Varonis, E., and S. Gass. 1985. Miscommunication in native/non-native conversation. *Language in Society* 14:327–43.

Vasquez, G. M., and M. Taylor. 1999. What cultural values influence American public relations practitioners? *Public Relations Review* 25:433–49.

Victor, D. A. 1992. *International Business Communication.* New York: HarperCollins.

Walker, B. A. 1991. Valuing differences: The concept and a model. In *Valuing Differences in the Workplace,* edited by M. A. Smith and S. J. Johnson. Alexandria, VA: ASTD.

Walker, B. A., and W. C. Hanson. 1992. Valuing differences at Digital Equipment Corporation. In *Diversity in the Work Place: Human Resource Initiatives,* edited by S. E. Jackson. New York: Guilford Press.

Watzlawick, P., J. Beavin, and D. D. Jackson. 1967. *The Pragmatics of Human Communication.* New York: W. W. Norton.

Weick, K. 1979. *The Social Psychology of Organizing.* 2d ed. Reading, MA: Addison-Wesley.

Wheeler, M. J. 1996. *Diversity: Business Rationale and Strategies.* New York: Conference Board.

White, C., and N. Raman. 1999. The World Wide Web as a public relations medium: The use of research, planning, and evaluation in Web site development. *Public Relations Review* 25:405–19.

Wilcox, D. L., P. H. Ault, and W. K. Agee. 1995. *Public Relations Strategies and Tactics.* 4th ed. New York: HarperCollins.

Wilmot, W. W., and J. Hocker. 1998. *Interpersonal Conflict.* 5th ed. Dubuque, IA: Wm. C. Brown.

Wilson, L. J. 1990. Corporate issues management: An international view. *Public Relations Review* 16:40–51.

Wiseman, R. L., ed. 1995. *Intercultural Communication Theory.* Thousand Oaks, CA: Sage.

Wiseman, R. L., and J. Koester, eds. 1993. *Intercultural Communication Competence.* Newbury Park, CA: Sage.

Wood, J. T. 1997. Diversity in dialogue: Commonalities and differences between friends. In *Communication Ethics in an Age of Diversity,* edited by J. M. Makau and R. C. Arnett. Urbana: University of Illinois Press.

World population hits 5.5 billion. 1992. *Lewiston Tribune,* 11 July, 2A.

Wouters, J. 1991. *International Public Relations: How to Establish Your Company's Product, Service, and Image in Foreign Markets.* New York: AMACOM, American Management Association.

Wylie, F. W. 1994. Commentary: Public relations is not yet a profession. *Public Relations Review* 20:1–3.

Index